GW00835885

A Tale of Two Captains

John Baynes
and
Hugh Maclean

A Tale of Two Captains

The Pentland Press Ltd.
Edinburgh

First published in 1990 by
The Pentland Press Ltd.
Kippielaw, Haddington,
East Lothian, Scotland.

Typeset by IPEK Origination
Printed & bound by Holmes McDougall (Edinburgh)
Jacket design by Ann Ross Paterson
ISBN 0 946270 78 3.

Dedicated to the memory of
the late Elizabeth Maclean Slayter
daughter of J.B. Maclean
and
the late Ethel Audrey Baynes
wife of R.M.S. Baynes

Contents

Preface

Although their two paths may never have crossed, and they
certainly never served together in the same battalion, the two
captains of this story were bound by the link which has such
strength for members of the British Army: they belonged to the
same regiment, The Cameronians (Scottish Rifles). All regiments
tend to use the same aphorism, but the saying has often been
repeated: 'Once a Cameronian, always a Cameronian'. It is
because of this indissoluble link that the sons of the two central
characters have combined to produce this book.

Each section has its own explanation, so at this stage only the
briefest outline of the book's structure is necessary. The first part
contains the memoirs of Captain Rory Baynes (later Lieutenant-
Colonel Sir Rory, Baronet), running from his birth in 1886 up to
1917. Dictated when he was in his eighties, and almost blind, these
memoirs give an interesting picture of life in late Victorian and
Edwardian times, as well as recounting his own experiences in the
First World War.

The second part consists of selections from the letters written by
Captain Joseph B. Maclean, M.C., from France and Flanders
during 1917 and 1918 to his brother Alexander T. Maclean, in
Springfield, Massachusetts, U.S.A. Serving with the 1st Battalion
of the regiment, Maclean, a Territorial officer, was at first a
platoon and then a company commander. His lettters, in this
edition largely unrevised, provide a detailed and dramatic insight
into life in the trenches as well as daily routine when out of the line,
in the last two years of the war. It is of particular interest that,
before returning to Britain to enlist in 1914, Maclean had been
laying the foundations of a most successful actuarial career in the
United States, where he had worked since 1911.

The editors of their fathers' writings have both seen military
service. John Baynes served for nineteen of his twenty-six years in
the army as a regular officer in The Cameronians (Scottish Rifles).
Hugh Maclean served from 1940 to 1946 with the Argyll and
Sutherland Highlanders of Canada (Princess Louise's) the 1st
Battalion and he wrote the war-time history of the regiment.

Rory Malcolm Stuart Baynes

At the end of 1908, as a newly commissioned regular 2nd Lieutenant in the Cameronians (Scottish Rifles).

Rory Malcolm Stuart Baynes

1886	Born at Reigate on 16 May.
1894-99	Hildersham Hall Preparatory School.
1899-1903	Harrow School
1906-08	3rd Bedford Militia
1908-12	1st Bn The Cameronians (Scottish Rifles) in India, South Africa and Glasgow.
1912-14	Sierra Leone Battalion, Royal West African Frontier Force.
1914-15	Adjutant, 9th Bn The Cameronians (Scottish Rifles). Wounded at Festubert in May 1915.
1915-16	Hospital and light duties.
1917-20	Sierra Leone Battalion, RWAFF.
1921-25	2nd Bn The Cameronians (Scottish Rifles).
1925-27	Commanding 2nd Nigeria Battalion, RWAFF.
1928-32	Second-in-Command, 1st Bn The Cameronians (Scottish Rifles).
1933-37	Commanding 2nd Bn The Cameronians (Scottish Rifles). Retired from active list in 1937.
1938-39	Chief Recruiting Officer, Scottish Command, as retired officer.
1940-41	Commanding Shetland Defence Battalion on recall to active duty.
1942-45	Supervising aerodrome defence in Orkney Islands, and then Home Guard training in Fife. Retired again July 1945. Settled near Bath, Somerset.
1947-59	Member Somerset County Council.
1960-70	Alderman on Somerset County Council.
1971	Succeeded as 6th Baronet of Harefield Place.
1972-79	Lived with his son at Lake Vyrnwy Hotel, Mid-Wales.
1979	Died on 29 April, shortly before his 93rd birthday.

The Memoirs of
Lieutenant Colonel Sir Rory Baynes, Bt

[Finding his eyesight failing when he was in his eighties, Sir Rory obtained a dictating machine, and was able to correspond with his son on tapes after he could no longer write or read letters. He was then persuaded to record, on his machine, his memories of his early life, and in all he dictated some 35,000 words over a period of two years. These reminiscences were typed out for him by a young lady living in the neighbourhood of Wellington, Somerset, where he had settled in the mid-sixties to live with his sister.

The memoirs which follow have been edited and shortened considerably, but still give an interesting picture of the life of a young man brought up in comfortable, though not lavish, circumstances in the late Victorian and Edwardian days when British power and wealth were at their zenith.

The baby to be christened in due course Rory Malcolm Stuart was born at South Park, Reigate on 16 May 1886. His father, the Reverend Malcolm Baynes, a younger son of Sir William Baynes, 3rd Baronet, was then a Curate in Reigate. His mother, Margarita, was the daughter of Canon Arthur Cazenove, the Vicar of the parish, and her eldest brother Arthur Philip Cazenove was a partner in the family firm of stockbrokers. Another brother, Walter, devoted his life to fox-hunting, being MFH in turn of the New Forest, Wilton, and Woodland Pytchley hounds. She had other brothers and sisters as well. Malcolm's eldest brother was a Bank of England agent, and among his other five brothers, there was a civil engineer, two soldiers – one in the 60th Rifles and one a Cameron Highlander – and two solicitors.

> *There was also one sister, but she was not allowed to*
> *marry the man she loved until after her father had*
> *died, when she was nearly sixty, because the family*
> *considered him an unsuitable match for her!*
> *The young Rory Baynes's story starts with early*
> *recollections of South Park, Reigate.]*

Early Years

There are four things I remember most clearly. One is a stuffed armadillo which was kept in the bottom of a cupboard in father's dressing room. The next, a monkey puzzle tree in the garden, and then a sword which mother bought for me. The fourth is Uncle Roddy staying, sitting on a seat in the garden and producing, in some most mysterious way, shillings out of pebbles, and from the leaves of a creeper on the house. I often wonder if these made such an impression on me because they were prophetic. The armadillo and the prickly monkey puzzle tree may have foretold my interest in chasing strange animals through thick, prickly African forests. The sword was, of course, for my interest in the army, and Uncle Roddy with the shillings would account for my always hopeful attitude towards financial difficulties, that some easy money will turn up.

When I was four or five, father was appointed rector of Crondall in Hampshire, where we lived for the next few years.

We were only a few miles from Aldershot, and quite often troops used to come through the village, so my enthusiasm for the army was kept up. I remember, on one occasion, a squadron of red coated cavalry coming by and I sat on the wall with my sword, saluting, and was happy to have my salutes returned. But best of all was a review at Aldershot in the presence of the Queen. I remember her very well, sitting in her carriage with a black bonnet on, looking rather square and forbidding. We went down in the four-wheeled dog cart which was drawn up to the ropes. The horses were removed and taken away somewhere at the back, and we sat and watched the review. It was a wonderful sight to see the cavalry, then all in full dress, first of all galloping past, next forming a line in the distance, and then charging down at the last moment in front of us.

I've got, somewhere, a photograph of myself in a sailor's suit with long golden curls. I disliked long hair for boys then just as much as I do now and managed to have them removed, but poor brother Keith had to keep his curls until sometime after we'd gone to Crondall. However, I dealt with the matter – I took him out into the garden one morning and cut them off. I don't think mother was very pleased.

We also used to go to stay with the Cazenove grandparents at Cranborne Manor, the lovely old Elizabethan house with all sorts of interesting things which Canon Cazenove rented for some years from the Marquess of Salisbury. I remember Queen Elizabeth's saddle, which was hanging up in the entrance hall. There were spiral stone staircases at each end leading to small turrets. I always remember Uncle Walter's room in one turret, as in a corner there was a sword and some polo sticks. I think he must have been in the 3rd Bedford Militia at that time, which was the regiment I joined later. Queen Elizabeth's room, where I sometimes slept, had an enormous four poster bed and behind the curtains at the back of it there was a hole in the wall, which was said to come out in one of the turrets. It was supposed to be a priest's hole, and I didn't much care about it when I was left alone at night. It was at Cranborne that grandfather Cazenove died. He dropped dead after finishing a game of tennis.

When I was just eight, I was sent to a preparatory school at Hildersham House, near Broadstairs. It was a new school and would now be considered a rather forbidding looking building, all rather new. There was no floor covering at all in the boys' part of the house, and we had four large dormitories with beds on either side and a row of wash basins down the centre; there was a little shelf above one's bed, but nowhere to put any belongings at all except in one's desk in the classroom, and that was very small too. In fact we weren't allowed any belongings, especially sweets. If any were brought back, they were all taken and doled out – one each after lunch on Sundays. I did not find out until sometime later that Grandmamma Baynes was always sending things like cakes from Buzzard's and all sorts of delicacies. These were also handed out occasionally. I had no idea I had anything to do with them and we all thought that they were due to the kindness of the Head-master.

Certainly my days at school were not the happiest days of my life. On the other hand, I think we enjoyed the holidays very much more after this restriction and discomfort. One thing I always remember was the shudder of excitement, or almost horror, that went through the school when a boy called Quin was beaten with a slipper for using bad language. The depraved boy was heard to say 'damn'!

It must have been in '97 that we moved to Ringwould. By that time Keith had come to Hildersham House and we heard nothing about the move at all until the middle of the term. At the end of term, instead of the usual journey to London and down to Farnham, father arrived in the four-wheeled dog cart with a pair of horses. I suppose they were given a rest for a time, and then he drove us back to Ringwould, a matter of some fifteen miles or so. This was a real thrill. Ringwould was a large Victorian rectory standing in three or four acres of grounds with a paddock; stables for three or four horses and a coachhouse; a large walled kitchen garden and lots of trees, shrubberies, etc. In fact, the sort of place children love. There was a footpath going out from the kitchen garden which joined up with the gardens of Ringwould House where the Monins lived. Joe Monins was the squire and owned most of the land round about. Mrs Monins was a Cobbold, and a cousin of mother's and they were the closest of friends. They had four children at the time – one boy and three girls, and we were all more or less the same family. Actually, with both of us usually having all sorts of other friends to stay during the holidays, we made rather a formidable gang.

This was about the time of the Mahdi rising in the Sudan. As Lord Kitchener, then Sir Herbert Kitchener, was a cousin of the Monins and was always in touch with them, we got a good deal of first class news about it. Most of our games, at that time, consisted of battles between the gallant British troops and the Dervishes. Being the eldest, I was always the gallant victorious British soldier and the enemy went down in rank according to their ages. All the small ones were Dervishes and made to charge with frightful war cries and fell in their hundreds – a frightful slaughter! After these successes I was more and more determined to become a soldier.

After the Mahdi rising and the retaking of Khartoum, we used to see quite a lot of Kitchener's staff, who used to come and stay at Ringwould House.

We were all very interested in cricket, and one of the great occasions was going to the Canterbury cricket week which always took place in the first week of August. First-class cricketers, especially members of the Kent XI, became new heroes. Of course, when the Boer War started, Generals became more important again. While Lord Salisbury was Prime Minister he was considered quite high up, almost equal to masters of foxhounds, but subsequent Prime Ministers didn't count. As to the standing of Generals and first-class cricketers, I think that depended very much on how either the war or the County Championships were

Rory Baynes aged 3.

Rory at Crondall, aged 11.

going. Archbishops had a certain position, and some Bishops, especially those who were personally known, such as the Bishop of Winchester, who used to give good children's parties at Farnham Castle during our time at Crondall.

I went to Harrow in the summer term of 1900 and, once more, I don't think I learned very much. I liked the arts school best and I liked Mr Hine the art master, and he seemed to like me. I always chose either drawing or painting for the holiday task, which we had to do every holidays, as opposed to reading a book on which one was examined at the end of the holidays. I was also good at anything which had an interesting story attached to it, and I remember on one occasion my Housemaster, at what was called 'pupil room', where most of the house assembled, stating that if they taught nothing at Harrow except Greek mythology, then Baynes would be top of the school. Very kindly, he didn't add that as it was Baynes was very nearly at the bottom. I did however, get one prize – I think they were called a 'try' – after which I was moved into a higher form, which was taken by Somervell, the man who taught Winston Churchill English. I joined the school Corps, so can claim to have served in the reign of Queen Victoria. We had a grey uniform with dark blue facings and silver buttons, and a little pill-box cap, worn on the side of the head with a black chin strap. Later I became a bugler, but I don't think I was ever capable of sounding a chord correctly, and altogether my military career at Harrow was certainly undistinguished. The first outstanding event whilst I was there was the 'relief of Mafeking' when the whole school turned out in the High Street, everybody cheering and shouting and throwing our straw hats high in the air. It must have been a wonderful day for the school store who supplied the hats. The next important event was the death of Queen Victoria, which occurred early in the morning on a day when I was going back to Harrow, and father sent me off to the Church to put the flag at half mast. We went up to London for the Queen's funeral, and I sat on a chimney pot on one of the small lodges beside the Mall to watch the procession go past. One had a very good view, and I got a clear impression of all the magnificent array of Kings, Princes and so on riding along behind the coffin. I particularly remember the Kaiser in a brilliant white and gold uniform.

The next Royal occasion was a sad disappointment. This was King Edward VII's coronation. We were all ready with royal purple handkerchiefs and ties, ready to go up for it, and then just before the day, he got appendicitis, and the whole thing was put off. When it eventually took place it was during the holidays so we didn't go.

Of course, one of the best occasions of all was the Eton and Harrow cricket match, and during the time that I was there Harrow won every year. This had nothing to do with me as my cricket was confined to one of the lower teams. Those of us in the lower school attended the match suitably dressed in Eton suits. I rather think this was white waistcoats, top hats, dark blue ties with a cornflower in our button hole and carrying a nice little stick with dark blue tassels tied on to it. The upper school wore morning coats, which had just then taken the place of the old frock coat. At the end of a very exciting finish, all the young gentlemen ran on to the ground where they started to bash in each others top hats with sticks, surrounded by a ring of laughing policemen holding hands; a most enjoyable occasion.

In 1901 it was observed when going to the Eton and Harrow match that many people were carrying rather heavier sticks than in the previous year. The hat bashing went very well and happily, but unfortunately the Headmasters and various other people took a dim view of it, and that was the last occasion on which it was permitted. Some people might have regarded this as an unwarranted outbreak of violence, but there was no malice about it, and it was all most enjoyable.

Ringwould Rectory.

As my school progress at Harrow had been slow – in fact, almost imperceptible! – I had to go to a crammer to prepare for the Army entrance exam. This 'forcing house' was at Smarden, in Kent, and it was run by the Reverend Collins, the vicar there, whose two sons, Percy and Keith, were both going into the Army. It was here that I had made up my mind that I would go in through the Militia. Percy Collins was already in the Militia, having joined the 3rd Battalion of the Buffs, and we visited him, both at the depot in Canterbury, and later on, when the Militia were training, down at Shorncliffe. I found that I much preferred the idea of sporting a militia officer's magnificent uniform, than the thought of going to Sandhurst, where in those days, I would have had to endure about two years in what was still rather a public school atmosphere.

In due course (i.e., some time in 1905), I managed to qualify in the Army entrance exam – though happily for me, not at the competitive level that would have gained me a place at Sandhurst. So my next stage was to join the Militia – which was what I had really wanted.

In order to get a regular commission via the Militia (which was my ultimate aim), I gathered that I would have to do a period of recruit training at a regimental depot; go to camp with the Militia for at least two periods of training of a month each; do an attachment of two or three months with a regular battalion; and then finally, pass the Militia Competitive examination. Although at that time, I could count on having about two years in which to prepare for that exam, I realised all the same, that it consisted solely of military subjects, in none of which I hitherto had the slightest grounding. I therefore went off straight away to learn about these from a Major Heath in Folkestone, who turned out to be a militia officer with a very imposing figure (he stood about 6ft. 2 ins.) with an upturned Kaiser moustache – the latter being a very popular form of adornment in military circles in those days. (But then, everything German – or everything connected with the German Army, anyway – was highly thought of, in that era). Heath was a type of man that I liked and respected and I soon found him to be an excellent teacher who made me very interested in all the subjects he taught. I luckily had a reasonable memory, and this proved to be quite useful, when during our military history lessons, we had to tackle such books as Hamley's *Operations of War*, and *Clausewitz on War*.

Though I got my first commission in the Militia (the 3rd Bedfords) in 1905, I remained based at Heath's until I had taken the exam for my regular commission in 1907.

The Bedford Militia

It had been through an uncle of mine, Walter Cazenove, that I had joined the 3rd Bedfords. He had been in that regiment himself, and he had married a girl called Dolly Higgins, whose brother was still serving in the Militia as a captain, and whose family had a large place at Turvey, only a few miles from Bedford. In those days, the 3rd Bedfords were a somewhat strange and exclusive crowd (as you will hear), and I don't think that anyone could have got into them without the prior approval of the Duke of Bedford himself. However, it seemed that Uncle Walter had managed to persuade the Duke to have me.

I well remember the arrival of my uniform at Ringwould and trying on the various things for the family to admire – full-dress, mess-kit, blue jumper and service-dress. I was rather disappointed at not having been allowed the frock coat – a long blue thing – but as they were never worn at training, and would in any case, have been quite useless afterwards, so far as I was concerned, it was probably just as well. For that matter, I don't think that I ever saw anybody else wear one.

In March or April 1906, I reported at the Bedford Regiment's depot for my recruit training. Kempston Barracks was a typical example of the Victorian type of barracks. Upon going through the main gate, one was faced with the barrack square, on the right of which were the officers' mess and their quarters, and on its left, the guardroom, orderly room, quartermaster's stores and various other buildings, all facing the square. Also on the left, and at right angles to these buildings, were the troops' barrack rooms. The remaining two sides of the square were bounded by a high red-brick wall. Although the officers' mess was quite comfortable and reasonably well furnished, the officers' quarters were not so inviting – though it never struck me at the time that they were in the least bit uncomfortable. In my mind's eye, I see a square room with a single window (the latter having a blind to it, but of course, no curtains); a bed; a chest-of-drawers with a mirror over it; a table; a wooden and hard-seated 'Windsor' chair; a wash-hand-stand with a jug and basin; a tin hip-bath; two candlesticks; and an uncarpeted rough board floor.

The recruit training was the responsibility of the regular depot staff, but always during this period, there were one or two attached militia officers who were what we used to call permanent militiamen. Some of them used to spend the whole year round

Rory outside his tent at militia camp, Ampthill Park, 1906.

With two other young militia officers (Rory in the centre).

going to various militia camps, attending these recruit training periods and being attached to regular units – thereby drawing pay for most of the year. One of these, when I first joined, was Dicky Knight who become one of my greatest friends.

Most of the training consisted of drill on the square, and musketry (later termed weapon drill). We were also taught the duties of an orderly officer, mess etiquette and various other odds and ends of that kind. For parade purposes generally, and for long periods of squad drill on the square, in particular, we were issued with a suit of rough canvas cloth which we wore over our other uniform. I used to think how glorious it must be, to be like Dicky Knight, who often supervised the parades and who marched up and down on his own dressed in his proper uniform, carrying a swagger-cane under his arm and making occasional comments. It wasn't till afterwards, when I had to do that sort of thing myself, that I realised what an appalling bore it was, that I came round to the view that one was really much happier after all, when actually taking part in the activities on the square – even if they only involved forming-fours, or turning to the right or left, or saluting with the one hand or the other, as we used to do in those days.

My first attempt as orderly officer was a bit of an ordeal, especially when it came to the business of going round the men's dinners and of asking whether there were any complaints. Fortunately, one was always accompanied by a senior orderly sergeant, who invariably knew the right answers. Thus it was, that on the first occasion, when my somewhat timidly-voiced 'Any complaints?' had immediately brought an old soldier to his feet, with the terse comment 'Spuds is bad, sir!', my escort had been ready for it and, much to my relief, had dealt with the situation both promptly and thoroughly. Incidentally, in those days, there were no such things as dining-halls, nor any other luxuries of that sort. The men had their meals in their own barrack-rooms, where beds were made up and were swung round against the walls, and where tables and F.F.F's (forms, folding, flat) were placed down the middle of the room.

By the time the recruit training had ended, our drill was not too bad – nothing like up to the Sandhurst form, of course, but nevertheless quite reasonable – and we had mastered the elements of rifle-shooting and of weapon-training generally, and had learned a certain amount on the miniature range. We had also had a fairly varied social life. There had been a certain amount of entertainment in the barracks and we had been invited out by many people in Bedford and round about.

It was about this time, that Dicky Knight had bought the famous (or anyway, locally famous) Panhard car, in which he and I toured the country during the next two years. It was an 8-horse-power, -2 cylinder affair, and was completely open – i.e., it didn't have a windscreen. Still, it was regarded as thoroughly up-to-date in 1906!

The Militia at Camp

My next bit of soldiering was when I accompanied the 3rd Bedfords to camp for their annual training. We had all mustered, to begin with, at Kempston Barracks, where we had spent a hectic day in issuing arms, equipment, etc. A business which had not been made any easier by the number of happy and enthusiastic drunks who had been among the militiamen reporting for duty! A fair number of the militia officers had lunched in the depot mess that day, but not all of them. Those who had refrained from doing so, had probably remained away, out of deference to the old Duke, who would never enter that mess, nor would have anything to do with its regular members. Apparently, some years earlier, a party of the regular officers from Kempston Barracks had been invited to a mess night in the 3rd Bedfords Camp. During the course of the evening, some of those guests had thought that it would be rather a joke to slip quietly out and let down the tents of some of their hosts. Unfortunately however, the joke had misfired, because it had turned out that the Duke's own tent had been among the flattened ones. Like Queen Victoria, 'he had not been amused!' – in fact, such was his displeasure, that he never forgave the perpetrators, nor any of the other regular officers who had followed them at Kempston Barracks.

Later in the afternoon, when things were reasonably under control, the battalion marched out to the railway station, where we entrained and travelled to Ampthill. There we detrained and marched to our camping ground in Ampthill Park. As this was the Duke's property, everything had naturally been done to made us comfortable in every way. A ridge ran up the centre of the park and it was on one of its gentle slopes that our camp had been erected. There, we found that a level plot had been cut out of the slope for each tent, and that water had been laid on, with taps at intervals. Our sleeping accommodation was in bell-tents, which had been furnished in very much the same way as our room in barracks, and the officers' mess had the appearance of a small canvas town, with

Militiamen drilling at Camp.

Duty in the butts at the rifle range – a job he did not enjoy!

several large marquees and a number of smaller tents of all shapes and sizes, all surrounded by canvas walls. Below the ridge was a very large level area, which provided us with a parade ground, and with plenty of space for our training generally.

Our training was mainly taken up with drill, and with the firing of the annual musketry course. Starting with a certain amount of squad drill and company drill, we very soon went on to battalion drill, which, as a result of the South African War, consisted mainly of our moving about in what was called 'artillery formation'. This involved our turning from quarter-column into lines of company columns at distances and intervals of so many paces respectively, and was regarded as a highly up-to-date, if somewhat complicated, manoeuvre. Most of the commands were given by Sergeant-Major Williams, an ex-guardsman, who could stand on the hillside above the parade, and could make himself heard at a distance of half-a-mile or more. He had an uncanny way too, of picking out almost any man in the battalion by name, at any range.

We also had a certain number of ceremonial parades in full-dress, but the most important part of the training had been the firing of the annual musketry course – and it was then that I met a rifle range for the first time, and learnt to hate it! I quite enjoyed the course from the firing point end, but we very junior subalterns had to spend hours and hours in the butts every day. Sitting there, watching the targets go up and down, ticking the bullet-holes and seeing them pasted up, and keeping the butt-registers marked up, had driven one almost mad! As there were no telephones, we were obliged to shout and wave flags every now and then to stop the firing while people popped-up from the butts to attend to the targets – and this naturally slowed up the whole business a lot.

At that time, the Militia had not long had their old falling-block Martinis replaced by the newer Lee Enfield rifles, and the 3rd Bedfords had an amusing story about my uncle Walter Cazenove's 'close shave' on the range. A man had been shooting very badly, so uncle had called him to his presence, and had told him to stand facing him. Then, taking a key-ring out of his pocket and holding it up to his own eye, uncle had ordered the man to aim his rifle at the key-ring and to take a snap-shot. The object of this would presumably have been a two-fold one. Firstly, to find out whether the man knew how to aim correctly, and secondly, whether he could squeeze the trigger without snatching at it and jerking his rifle. The soldier duly raised his rifle and took aim, but made no attempt to pull the trigger. Whereupon Uncle Walter said 'Go on! Do what I told you! Snap your trigger!' but the man said 'No Sir! I won't'; once again Uncle Walter had repeated his order: 'Go on! Do what you're told!' to which the man had replied 'No Sir! I can't! It's loaded!'.

In due course, the less pleasant parts of the training (i.e., those wearisome hours in the butts) came to an end, and the battalion went on manoeuvres for a day or two – known then as field days. Those exercises must have been very simple ones, of course – i.e., when viewed in the light of modern developments – but they nevertheless had the effect then, of making us feel more like soldiers who were ready for battle.

In those more simple times, most of our militiamen would spend their evenings out visiting the local pubs, where quite a few of them appeared to regard it as the height of enjoyment to drink themselves into a stupor as speedily and thoroughly as possible. Not much notice was taken of those who could make their own way back to camp, and whose noisy songs were cheerful, as they staggered off to their tents. But those who looked like being troublesome in any way, were seized and frog-marched to the guard tent, where, on the occasions when its accommodation had become overcrowded, the most obstreperous of the detainees would be taken outside and pegged down – i.e. would be stretched out flat on the ground, with their arms and feet tied to tent-pegs. This simple expedient was regarded as quite normal in those days, and none of its victims seemed to resent it in any way. Although junior subalterns did not attend the orderly room when the Commanding Officer was dealing with these offenders, we were responsible for entering up the punishment afterwards, in the defaulters' sheets concerned (or conduct sheets, as they have since been known). So far as I can remember, those punishments were almost entirely in the form of fines.

The officers' mess was most impressive. The P.M.C. was Lord Abinger (known as 'The Bean' – so called because he always liked a beano on any possible occasion!). In order to ensure that he had all his home comforts, and that he could maintain a suitable standard of living while he was in camp, 'The Bean' had brought his steward and a lot of his own staff with him, to run the mess. Hence it looked like a large canvas town. It was certainly all very good, but as our messing cost us 12s 6d a day, it was really rather expensive – particularly in the light of the fact that in those days you could get lunch at any first-class restaurant in London for 2s 6d, and a very good dinner for 5s! The mess silver was well up to standard and, in fact, there were several really fine pieces of silver and gilt. We had a piano in the ante-room tent, which Dicky Knight and various others used to play, and which in the evenings after dinner, was invariably surrounded by a large gathering of people who sang all the popular songs from the latest musical comedies. 'The Bean' was an enthusiastic performer on these occasions.

At my first camp, another peer, Lord Ampthill, who recently had been Governor of Madras, came to the training as a junior captain. Having been living in regal state in Madras, he had quite forgotten that in the Militia, a junior captain was not viewed as a person of any great importance. While he had been playing bridge one evening, at one end of the ante-room marquee, the usual singing and piano-playing had started up at the other end. That singsong had no sooner got under way, than his Lordship shouted out, 'Stop all that noise down there!'. Almost before he knew what had happened, he and some of his fellow bridge-players had found themselves sprawling on the floor beneath their bridge-table, with half the remaining furniture of the mess piled on top of them! We never had any more trouble from him after that – well, anyway, not until he eventually became Second-in-Command.

The Duke himself, didn't dine in the mess very often, but even when he did, things seemed to go on just as heartily as at any other time – though it is true, that his presence tended to be a bit unnerving if you happened to be the orderly officer that day. After attending the tattoo roll-call, the orderly officer, wearing cap and sword, had to come into the mess, salute the senior officer present , and report the number of men who had been found absent. There were usually quite a number of these. In fact, on most evenings there would probably be anything from, say, thirty to sixty men who had failed to return to camp by the appointed time – but then, these would only be temporary absentees who invariably reported back in due course. On one occasion however, when the Duke was dinning-in and I happened to be the orderly officer, the number of men who were still out, was anything but normal. Indeed, it was a very worried young officer who saluted the Duke that night, and who had to report: '360 men absent Sir!' Actually he took it very well.

There was only one other occasion, I think, when I ever had cause to feel really uncomfortable in the presence of the Duke, and when I had in fact, come pretty close to incurring his displeasure. I had a boomerang, which I used to throw about on the parade ground. As I simply hadn't any control over the thing, however, I never really had the faintest idea of what it would do next. Indeed, its flight was most erratic, and it did all sorts of interesting things. Well, one day, when I was amusing myself in this way, who should appear on the parade ground and begin to pace solemnly across it, than the Duke himself and Colonel James, the Second-in-

Command! I had just thrown the boomerang in what I had thought would be a perfectly safe direction, and had been hoping that it would return to me. Imagine my horror and dismay therefore, when I saw it literally chasing them across the parade ground at about knee height! I let out a piercing howl, which luckily warned them of their danger in time, and enabled them to leap smartly to one side. Needless to say, it was immediately brought to my attention in no uncertain manner, that while swords and revolvers were considered to be suitable weapons for militia officers, boomerangs were not!

While the 3rd Bedfords were in camp, a party of its officers was always invited to lunch by a Mr Anthony Wingfield, an exceedingly rich man, who lived in a large and magnificent house outside Ampthill, and who kept a wonderful private zoo in his very extensive grounds. Everything there was laid on in the most lavish style. On our arrival, our hats and sticks were taken by six footmen who were standing three a side on the steps leading up from the front door. At the top of these steps were two black-coated gentlemen who then took charge of us, and conducted us to the room in which our host and hostess were waiting to receive us. Lunch was positively sumptuous and must have consisted of some sixteen courses, of which a water-ice – just to cool things off – had been about the eighth! A veritable colony of different glasses had been laid alongside each place, and a succession of wines served to fill them.

At one of those lunches, Wingfield had had the Landgraf of Hesse staying with him – a minor German royalty whom 'The Bean' also knew well, and always called the 'Land Crab'. Like most of the German feudal lords of that day, the 'Land Crab', who was nearly blind, liked nothing better than the spectacle of large masses of scarlet-clad troops marching about on parade. It is to be hoped, therefore, that he felt duly flattered when we went to the trouble of laying on a special ceremonial parade for him.

Sumptuous though Anthony Wingfield's lunches were they were nothing compared to the dinners at Woburn Abbey! Our mess kits, which we always wore when dining there, added to the colour of an already colourful scene. Behind every chair there would be a footman in magnificent livery, and at intervals of every two or three chairs, there would be other gentlemen in black coats, to pour out the wine. Down the centre of the table, would be a variety of gleaming gold plate, and all our food was served on solid silver plates. Although there were not so many courses as at Wingfield's – about eight to ten, I should say – there were just as many different wines. With the coffee and liqueurs, we were given magnificent cigars, the smoking of which was a real treat – and would have been even more so, if we had ever been given the chance to smoke them to the end! Unfortunately, however, when dinner was finished, we were always taken up a broad flight of stairs to the billiard tables in an upper gallery, where smoking was not permitted. Two footmen each carrying an enormous silver tray, were always stationed on each side of the bottom step of that great stairway and, much to our dismay, we all had to deposit our lovely cigars on those trays – having only had time to enjoy the first inch or so, of those six-inch beauties! I can still remember how shocked and disappointed I was, the first time this happened to me, and how envious I was of the Duke's menservants who presumably finished the things off for us!

Some of us were also invited to lunch at Woburn, but these were not nearly such formal affairs. Indeed, I can still picture the old Duke, standing in front of the fire in his small smoking-room before lunch, with a greasy and perfectly dreadful old cloth cap pulled down over one eye. But then, it was his custom to wear each of his many and various forms of headgear, cocked over one eye like that – including his helmet on a ceremonial parade. After lunch, we were sent round the park to have a look at the animals, and as it was said not to be altogether safe to wander amongst the gnus and the odd buffalo or two, which roamed the grounds, we were driven there in vehicles which must have been examples of the very earliest attempts to produce what came to be known as motor vehicles. Could anyone see those quaint-looking machines today, he might be excused for supposing that they had been designed by one of Heath Robinson's forebears.

Besides being invited to the Wingfield's and to Woburn Abbey, we also used to be entertained by quite a number of the other people round about. In return, we used to give two large parties in Camp for the local nobility and gentry. These parties always started off with a ceremonial parade, which was then followed by a sort of garden party in the afternoon.

Soon after Camp was over I was due to set out for my period of attachment to the 2nd Battalion of the Bedfordshire Regiment at Bordon, in Hampshire.

With a Regular Battalion
at Bordon

The collective training season had started when I got to Bordon, so during my stay there, I not only learnt quite a lot about matters of general regimental routine, which proved useful to me when I eventually joined the Cameronians, but I also took part in the company and battalion training schemes. Afterwards I accompanied the battalion on brigade exercises and manoeuvres at a higher level. I also found out what it was like to march for mile after mile, wearing full marching order, along straight and dusty roads which seemed to have no end. I savoured that wonderful moment when the troops had at last been dismissed, and one could stagger back to the mess to find the mess sergeant waiting there, with a tray of glasses and a large jug of shandy!

My two chief friends of the 2nd Bedfords, were Foss, who later won the V.C. in the 1914-18 War, and McIvor Cranko, who was training to enter the Army Boxing Championships.

Soon after that, I was joined at Bordon by another 3rd Battalion militiaman, the Earl of Seafield. He had been in the 3rd Bedfords for several years, but I had not met him before.

Just before the end of my attachment to the 2nd Bedfords, the Bordon Garrison gave a one-night Torchlight Tattoo. I think that it must have been one of the first of its kind. Anyway, instead of it including all kinds of displays, which are now a recognised feature of modern Military Tattoos, it was largely a spectacle of the drill movements to be seen on a parade ground (but with all the men carrying flaming torches), and of the marching and counter-marching of Military Bands. All the same, it was really quite effective.

Looking back on that period of training at Bordon, it afterwards struck me that, in all the weeks I had spent there, no one had ever said anything to me about the importance of looking after the welfare of the troops – and yet, it was the first thing that had been impressed upon me, when I had joined the Cameronians. True, I had been made to go round the men's dinners in Bordon, to see if there were any complaints, and I had also been told how important it was to hold regular inspections of their kit and barrack-rooms, to ensure that they were keeping their clothing in good order and their premises clean and tidy. But no one had given me to understand that it was an officer's first duty to take a personal interest in the men under his command, and to make it his business to see that they were being properly looked after.

No sooner had I arrived in the Cameronians however, than I was told straightaway, that an officer must always put the interests and well-being of his men before his own. I quickly learnt for instance, that no officer should ever dream of taking off his own equipment, or of going to his own tent, or of having a meal after returning to camp or bivouacs, no matter how weary he himself might feel, until he had first seen for himself, that all his troops had been adequately accommodated and fed. And it was made clear to me moreover, that officers should do this, not merely because it happened to be an order, but rather, because the well-being of their men should be a matter of genuine concern to them at all times.

Awaiting a Regular Commission

After the annual training in 1907, I sat the Militia Competitive exam, in order to gain a regular commission. For this exam I went to stay in London with my uncle Christy Baynes, who was agent for the Bank of England at Temple Bar. He had a large house above the Bank, where everything was very well done, and where there was always a footman available, to take you up and down in the lift. Uncle Christy was an enthusiastic golfer, but not, I think, a very good one. On Sunday mornings during my stay there, we used to go down into the Bank and, using corks for balls, we used to play shots off a mat at one end of the premises. The great thing was to hit a shot far enough to hit a clock at the far end. His home was certainly a very comfortable place in which to stay, and his sons had what almost amounted to a flat of their own, on the second or third floor up, where we young men all lived; only coming down to the more magnificent and austere apartments for meals. About the second day of the examination, I wasn't very well – having caught what I suppose would now be called a slight touch of flu. However, I managed to struggle through the rest of the papers.

Having sat for my exam, my time was free, so I went to stay with my Uncle Walter Cazenove at Langley Manor, where he had become Master of the New Forest Hounds and, there too, everything was done on a very lavish scale. It was while I was there, that we heard, much to everyone's surprise – except that of my tutor Major Heath – that I had passed out top in the Militia Competitive, and by a very fair margin of marks. Heath was delighted, and made it

the occasion for boosting his establishment by putting adver-
tisements in all the educational journals, proclaiming the results.
All I had to do then was to sit back and await my being gazetted to
a regiment. This suited me very well.

My name had been down for the Buffs. As that was the East
Kent Regiment, and the one therefore that belonged to our part of
the world, we had known a lot of its members, and so it had seemed
the natural thing for me to try for them. But nothing more had happened about it. The next thing was, that General Sir Leslie Rundle
(who had recently been Constable of the Tower at Dover, and who
was a great friend of ours) had asked me why I hadn't been gazetted. To which I had replied that I couldn't think why. Whereupon,
he paid a visit to the War Office to inquire about it for me, and had
come back to tell me that there were three choices open to me;
namely, that I could have a commission in the 60th (King's Royal
Rifle Corps), or the Seaforth Highlanders, or The Cameronians
(Scottish Rifles). As it seemed however, that you would have to
have a private income of at least £300 a year, to be able to exist in
either the 60th or the Seaforth, and as it was made amply clear to
me moreover, that my father didn't at all appreciate the idea of
providing me with anything like that amount, we naturally selected the Cameronians – which, after all, appeared to be a very good
compromise between the Cameron Highlanders and the 60th, in
which my father's two brothers, Kenny and Gillie had respectively
served. [£150 a year was expected in the Cameronians.]

While awaiting results, I had a very quiet and leisurely time, and
in fact, it was not until I was doing my annual training in the
Militia in 1908, that I was actually gazetted to the Cameronians. It
was then, incidentally, that I had the happy experience of drawing
pay from two sources at the same time, over a period of about ten
days or so. In other words, I was paid both as a militiaman, and as
a regular officer. What's more, they never recovered it from me – a
matter of which I have always been very proud. That was the year
when the Militia came to an end, and the Territorial Force (as it
was first called) was formed. This was announced on a parade, and
everyone was asked whether he wished to join the Territorials or
not. As a guide, they were told what their officers were going to do,
and Stephens, the Adjutant, told me afterwards, that when he had
read out that Lieutenant Baynes had obtained a regular commission, he had seen me suddenly pull myself taller by at least three
inches! And talking of Stephens, reminds me of one of the odd
ways in which things were done in those days. No sooner had the
3rd Bedfordshires ceased to exist as a militia regiment, than our
friend Stephens had suddenly made the remarkable jump from

having been a mere Captain in that regiment, to become Chief Constable of Bedfordshire.

Although I had been gazetted to the Cameronians I had been given the honour of carrying the regimental colour of the Bedford Militia, on the last parade of that regiment through the streets of Bedford town, to where the Colour had been laid up in a local Church. That had been a very hot day, and my full-dress uniform, with its strapped overalls and rather tight wellingtons, had made it a not altogether happy experience, although of course, a proud one.

A Short Stay with the 2nd Scottish Rifles in Aldershot

Although I had actually been gazetted to the 1st Battalion of the Cameronians, then in Cawnpore, I first had to spend a short time with the 2nd Battalion in Aldershot to await a troopship for India. Incidentally, in that day and age, one had to be particularly careful only to refer to our 2nd Battalion as the Scottish Rifles – i.e., without any mention of the title Cameronians.

I think that it must have been at the end of July, or at the beginning of August, that I arrived at Talavera Barracks in Aldershot, to report to the 2nd Scottish Rifles. It was shortly after lunch, I seem to remember, when I walked timidly into the ante-room of the officers' mess, to find that its only other occupant was a man sitting in a deep armchair, with a newspaper over his face. On my entry, the newspaper had been lowered slightly, and first to come into view, were a pair of large and beetling black eyebrows. Next I saw a pair of glaring eyes, and a voice from behind the newspaper, barked: 'What are you? Visitor, or come to join?'. I timidly said 'Come to join'. Whereupon up went the newspaper again and that was the end of that! The man behind the newspaper was Maxwell Henning, father of the young Bill Henning who subsequently joined the Regiment, and who eventually became a Brigadier. Needless to say, I got it back on young Bill years later – but that is another story.

In those days of course, a newly joined Second Lieutenant was looked upon as less than the dust, so this was a valuable lesson for me, because, having had my second 'pip' in the Militia, and having carried the Colours, and so on, I've no doubt that I had been getting a bit self-important.

In September I sailed for India on the troopship *Rohilla,* which left from Southampton. I had stayed the night before with Uncle Walter at Langley and he and Aunt Dolly had come to see me off.

The Journey to Cawnpore

As troopships went, the *Rohilla* was quite a comfortable one, with plenty of deck space. I don't remember anything particular about that voyage, except going ashore for a look round when we got to Port Said. My memory tells me that it was then a very tumble-down sort of place with no decent buildings, and where there were sandy tracks instead of roads.

When we arrived at Karachi – another very unimpressive place – we all disembarked there. Most of the passengers appeared to be going to the North West Frontier or to other stations in Northern India, and they continued their journeys, I think , by train. Those of us however, who were going to the United Provinces, or to Central India, re-embarked on a small coastal steamer, and went down to Bombay, where, on finding that we were going to have to spend two or three days there, before being sent on to our various destinations, we stayed at the Taj Mahal Hotel. The Taj probably was, and perhaps still is, the best hotel in India – and yet, it can't have been unduly expensive in those days, or we couldn't possibly have afforded to stay there. As far as I can remember, our principal fare in that hotel, consisted of foie gras and cocktails, but as soon as we started the long hot train journey to Cawnpore, we had to accustom ourselves to Indian cooking. The train stopped at intervals for our meals, which were taken in the station restaurants – always full of flies and strange smells. After spending one night on the train, we eventually reached Cawnpore on the following evening.

With the 1st Battalion in Cawnpore

We were met at the station by Tom Riddell-Webster (later General Sir Thomas), who must have been orderly officer that day, I think, and he had a strange kind of transport waiting for us. Upon reaching my bungalow, I went up some steps on to a sort of verandah, and had just pushed open some double doors into a room beyond, when I was met by a large bulldog which, despite been tied to a bedstead, was towing the thing across the room towards me, and growling at me in a horribly menacing way. In due course, I was told that this inside room belonged to one Tommy Dodd and that the verandah itself was to be my room. On looking round it, I found that it was furnished with a wooden bedstead that had string strung across it, by way of springs (such contraptions were known as 'charpoys'); a chair; a rickety table; and a large and equally rickety cupboard. I was told that if I wanted any other furniture, I would be able to hire it from the bazaar. At the end of the verandah was my 'gussilkhana', or bathroom. This contained a zinc tub and a table on which was a basin. I had been found a very good bearer, who had been sent down to Bombay to meet me. In a very short time he had got my things unpacked, had made the bed and had somehow managed to make the verandah seem inhabitable – such was the amazing way of Indian servants. Not long after, however, I was given a room inside the bungalow, as well as the verandah.

Sharing a bungalow with Tommy Dodd, although amusing in its way, had certain disadvantages. Tommy never seemed to have any clothes of his own and was always borrowing mine. What's more, he never bothered to ask before taking them. Having a fairly well-equipped subaltern as his stable-companion was just the thing he required. My bearer however, was a very good watch-dog and kept a close guard over my things. In fact, I think that he made it a routine to search Tommy's room every day, and to recover anything of mine that he found there.

James Jack had just become Adjutant, and such was promotion in 1908, that he was still a Second Lieutenant. [Not many years afterwards Jack became a Brigadier-General in the Great War, and the personal diaries which he so meticulously kept have been published as a book]. In those days, drill was considered to be all-important, but James Jack was a real addict. In fact it was almost a religion to him. Second Lieutenants on joining, no matter what their previous experience, had to be put on the square until they had been passed out by the Adjutant. Although I had completed my recruit training in the Militia; had attended three annual periods of training; had been attached to a regular battalion; and had got my second'pip' while I had been with the 3rd Bedfords; back I went on the square again. I was put under the charge of the Drill Sergeant, a first-class man named Henderson, whom I liked very much. Some years later, when I became Adjutant of our 9th Battalion, I was instrumental in getting him promoted to Company Sergeant Major. Although Henderson was perfectly satisfied by my performance, it was quite a while before James Jack would pass me off the square. What lay behind it all, I think, was that James rather liked exerting his authority, and therefore enjoyed having plenty of young officers at his beck and call on drill parades. Being only a Second Lieutenant himself however, the only officers he could order to attend his Adjutant's parades, were those who were junior to him.

There were eight companies in a battalion in those days, each commanded by a Major or Captain – though in practice they were probably more often left in the charge of subalterns. I was in 'B' Company, commanded by Major Vanderleur, of whom I saw very little. When he was in Cawnpore, he certainly showed up very seldom in barracks, and was always sending me notes, telling me to do all sorts of odds and ends. The Commanding Officer of the battalion, was Jerry McCann, who must have been the scruffiest officer that the regiment ever had. His uniform looked as if it were falling to pieces and there were large holes in his breeches, which were covered in stains and goodness knows what. Indeed, it was because his own doublet was in such a shocking state, that we were never paraded in full-dress, but used to wear our black patrol jackets on ceremonial parades instead. His chief interest was polo; he was an enthusiastic and quite good player. On battalion parades, he always had his polo ponies led round the outside of the parade ground, and spent most of his time looking at them. It was alleged, that on one such occasion, when he himself had been drilling the battalion, his attention had wandered for a moment to his ponies, and that before he had realised what was happening, the whole parade had marched straight into a wall, where its ranks had concertinaed and all had been chaos for a while. Although he was so careless in many ways and untidy, some of his ideas were well in advance of the times. He owned one of the only two or three cars to be seen in Cawnpore then, and on his last home leave he got married. In order to make his new wife feel more at home, and to provide her with rather better washing facilities than were to be found in the somewhat primitive 'gussilkhanas' of that era (which, as I have already explained, consisted of nothing more than a tin bathtub in a small cubicle), he had a proper bath, with hot and cold taps installed. Outside his bungalow, and connected to those bath-taps, he had two tanks erected: one for the cold water supply and the other to be filled by the 'bhisti' (i.e., the native water-carrier, with the goatskin bag, who used to be among the employees in every household) just before the 'memsahib' was going to have her bath. So she was able to enjoy the almost unheard-of luxury in any private residence in the India of those days, of being able to go into her bathroom and turn on the taps.

Our barracks in Cawnpore covered a considerable area. There were about a dozen large, grey, single-storey buildings, which had been there at the time of the Mutiny, more than fifty years earlier. The officers' mess and most of our bungalows were near the bank of the River Ganges, anything from half to three quarters of a mile away from the men's quarters, offices, and parade grounds, and bicycles were therefore our chief means of getting about – or, perhaps, I should say the chief means of the subalterns, because quite a few of the Captains and Majors possessed things called 'tum-tums' by which I mean a sort of two-wheeled dog-cart. A bicycle for example, was essential for the orderly officer, who had to visit and turn out several widely separated guard posts. There was the regimental quarter-guard in the barracks; another at the station magazine, which was a considerable distance from the barracks; and another at the Government Harness and Saddle Factory which was nearer the town, and which must have been about two and a half miles away. Things wouldn't have been too bad if we had not been continually troubled with punctures, but most of the roads there were bordered by some infernal kind of tree (the name of which I never discovered) that shed a strange and horrible seed in the shape of a small ball with very sharp spikes sticking out all round it – so that whichever way the seed fell, some of its spikes were always sticking upwards. These were called 'chipidusters', and nothing was more infuriating than to hear the hissing of your tyre, as it picked one of them up, when, accompanied by the orderly sergeant, you were wearily pedalling by night to visit the guard at the Harness and Saddle Factory, all dressed in you mess kit, with a sword dangling at your side, and doing your best to hold a hurricane lamp on your continually jerking handlebars, to light your way. The danger of getting your sword entangled in the spokes of your bicycle, and of you therefore being pitched headlong on to the dusty road, was enough of a hazard as it was, without getting a puncture into the bargain.

On my first Christmas at Cawnpore, I was invited to dinner with the McCanns and James Jack was there too. As we departed at about midnight, after quite a good evening, James Jack said to me 'You're orderly officer aren't you?' and I said 'Yes'. Whereupon he said 'Well, I think that this would be a very good night to turn out the Guards'!! – the exclamation marks are mine.

Another duty which sometimes fell to the lot of the orderly officer, was to supervise the bottling of the sergeants' mess whisky, which was imported in barrels containing, I think, enough to fill about 360 bottles. The bottling was done in a fairly small shed, which had a very low roof, and was extremely hot. The task was undertaken by two sergeants, one of whom filled the bottles and banged in the corks, while the other stood by with a pot of boiling sealing-wax ready to dab the stuff over the corks – all of which had to be done in the presence of the orderly officer. So 'heady' were the whisky fumes in that hot confined space, that by the time the business had been completed, it was just about all we could do to stagger blindly out of the shed.

Company commanders seldom worried about such nonsense as 'Company training'. Hence, the tackling of that task was generally left to the subalterns. The battalion's eight companies were normally paired together for such training, and at my first camp, about seven miles outside Cawnpore, 'A' Company (commanded by Tommy Dodd) and 'B' Company (commanded by myself), went there together. Between us, Tommy and I laid on the most amusing exercises that we could devise, and I think they were thoroughly enjoyed by everyone who took part in them. One exercise that I particularly remember, involved scrambling down some cliffs to the bank of the Ganges and embarking in boats to get over to the other side. The thing that added interest to the proceedings, was finding the water's edge littered with a mass of skulls and bones – the result of the Hindu custom of burning their dead on the banks of the Ganges and then pushing the half-consumed corpses into the water to be chewed up by turtles, crocodiles and so on. I imagine that some eddy must have washed up those gruesome remains at the particular point which we had chosen for our embarkation. At any rate the troops were immensely pleased.

Later, there were other forms of training, at which company commanders were expected to be present. The first of these, was the Kitchener Test which had been introduced by that famous soldier when he had been Commander-in-Chief in India. It consisted of a march in full marching order, of 15 miles, followed up by an attack across country, of another five miles. This all had to be done in a limited time; though what that time was, I can no longer remember. Marching along the Grand Trunk Road in those days, loaded with one's full equipment, was no laughing matter. That road was straight for miles and miles and there was so much dust that it was only possible to see about one rank in front of you. It certainly meant that a battalion was in fairly good condition if it could get to the end of that fifteen miles and then carry out an attack over another five miles, without losing more than two or three of its men on the way.

On these, as on all other training occasions, officers had to carry full water-bottles but weren't allowed to drink from them. As I mentioned in my first instalment of these memoirs, at all halts for meals, or for any other reason, no officer was allowed to take off his own equipment until he'd seen that all his men were comfortably settled down, had removed their equipment and were getting their food. I think, in this respect, we were rather in advance of some other regiments.

The training season used to finish with what I think were probably called command manoeuvres, when we all went down to the neighbourhood of Benares and took part in a continuous battle exercise for a period of three or four days. This was the first time that I had met with the business, to which one was to become well accustomed later on, of having to advance, while closely covered (occasionally too closely) by one's own artillery, whose shells not only dropped very near us but every now and again behind us. My most vivid memory, however, of my first manoeuvres, is of its climax. The bugles all sounded the officers call – which, as you know, is 'officers come and be damned' – and very soon, senior officers and their staff were to be seen coming from various directions and converging at some point nearby. Commanders out there were always followed in those days by a lancer with a pennant, and just as two or three of them had met opposite us, and we were all riding along and chatting together, a very fine, warrantable boar jumped up. Immediately, the commanders seized the lances of their orderlies, other officers drew their swords and, with one accord, they all galloped off after the pig, and away from the point at which they were supposed to be assembling. In other words they were damned if they were going to be 'damned', so to speak, until after they had got their pig.

Of course, those were the days that Kipling wrote about, and as a newly joined subaltern you could learn quite a lot from your first visit to India. The people who really taught us were the warrant officers and the senior N.C.O.'s, and they really were a splendid lot. The regimental sergeant-major was called Hamilton and although he was a small man, he was very dignified and had immense authority. The eight company sergeant-majors were always ready to help and advise, and most of them had a tremendous sense of humour. A sergeants' mess 'smoker' was subsequently remembered, not only for the 'head' you had next morning, but for the cheerful and delightful evening it had been. Pipe-Major Thorburn instructed us in highland dancing, or rather, he piped, while some of the more active members of the pipe band taught us the steps. I also did some boxing with Sergeant Winderham, the gym instructor, but the trouble with him was that although I was able to hit him quite frequently, I would almost have preferred to hit a good solid brick wall. I have never known anybody quite so tough.

I don't think that we used to take part in games with the men in those days, so much as we did later on, but I do remember having played in the regimental hockey team, and having gone to Allahabad for the All-India Hockey Tournament. That I think, must have been at the end of 1908 or early in 1909, and our week in Allahabad was a very cheerful one. There were celebrations every night for the teams who had been knocked out, and who could therefore afford to relax. They came from all over India, and included Gurkhas from the north, and goodness knows who from the south. The tournament was eventually won that year, by the Connaught Rangers – a regiment who didn't play hockey so much as that Irish game, which I think is called 'hurley', and which just means bashing your way, regardless, through all opposition. It was about this time that I had my first attack of malaria. There was a lot of it about and, in fact, we used to have 'quinine parades' two or three times a week. At these parades the whole of one's company had to march past the company sergeant-major, who put a spoonful of quinine in every man's mouth, while another N.C.O. was at hand with a mug of water, which he poured into the recipient's mouth to wash the nasty stuff down.

Polo in Cawnpore (1909-1910)

There was a generally understood classification of regiments in India before the First World War, based on one important point, and that was, that regiments who played polo all came at the top. All Indian Cavalry played polo but, I think, few infantry, although there were a certain number of individual polo players from various infantry regiments.

We were the only British regiment in Cawnpore. There were the Indian Cavalry, Hodson's Horse and one, or possibly two Indian infantry battalions, but we didn't see much of them. Some distance away from the army cantonment were the civil lines, occupied by civil servants; business men, generally called 'boxwallahs'; and a good many government officials connected with the Government Harness and Saddle Factory, and things of that kind. The place where all these men met was the club, which was in the cantonment, and was the centre of all social life, games, etc.

Of course, one of the first things I wanted to do was to get a polo pony, and this was possible owing to the regimental polo club, from which I borrowed sufficient money to buy a good steady old grey polo pony called'Cloibe'. He knew the game well and was most suitable for a beginner. I also got a reversed-hide saddle, etc. Although I'd been riding on and off since the age of four, I'd never been through a riding school and learnt their methods, so I managed to arrange to go through a course with Hodson's Horse recruits. Their method was to put you on a horse on a blanket, trot you round the manege until your legs were so tired that they were hanging limply down on either side and then put you over jumps. You were not allowed to touch the reins. When your balance was sufficiently improved to go over the lane of jumps without falling off, the next stage was to do the same thing but in this case on a new and rather shiny saddle without stirrups. It was not until you passed this stage that you were allowed to touch the reins and get on to the more difficult arts of horsemanship. It really taught one balance, which was very useful, especially playing polo.

There was very good duck shooting around Cawnpore but it used to take some time to get out to these places and we usually went out for two or three days and went into camp. Cawnpore was also famous for the pigsticking and large numbers came to the Cawnpore Tent Club. I never did any pigsticking myself as a polo pony was far too valuable to risk galloping over rough country and I hadn't got anything else to ride. After polo and other games everybody used to gather at the club, and there was all sorts of entertainment: dinner parties; dances, etc., and here again I started acting – amateur theatricals being very popular.

It was at the races that we did most of our entertaining and returned some of the hospitality we received. We had very few married officers and indeed getting married was quite unpopular. On first joining I was made to sign a paper saying that if I got married before I reached the rank of Captain I'd pay £50 to the mess; so although we couldn't entertain personally the best thing to do was to invite everybody to a large tent at the various race meetings. This was done very well indeed thanks very largely to the mess sergeant – Sergeant Goodwin – who was really a first-class man. On guest nights in mess he was like a very good butler with a large number of footmen at his disposal, but on these occasions at the racecourse he was much more like the steward of a ducal household.

As my polo improved I sold 'Cloibe' and got a first-class old mare called 'Hester'. She was no longer up to tournament form although I expect she had been in the past – but was just what I

RORY MALCOLM STUART BAYNES

wanted. She did me very well until I left India.

The Hill Station at Chakhrata

At the beginning of the hot weather a good many of the troops, especially those who had recently come out and were not really acclimatised, were sent up to the hills. We went to a place called Chakhrata about 8000 feet up from Dehra Dun. There was a permanent garrison at Chakhrata and that year the Lancashire Fusiliers were there. Detachments from various regiments all met at Dehra Dun and we went off for the three-day march up to the hills to Chakhrata. There were detachments of half a dozen or more regiments; we were the only Scottish one and there were also the Royal Irish. I can't remember all the others – I think there were the East Yorks, the South Staffords and one or two more. Transport was pack-mule and bullock cart. The lines occupied by visitors from the hot south were at Kailana about two miles along a ridge from Chakhrata. The barracks were at the top of the ridge and the officers' mess quarters some 200 feet or more below, facing north to the Himalayas. I shall never forget my first view of the Himalayas proper. The high peaks were often covered with cloud. One always expected to look out and just see this row of snow-capped mountains in the distance but suddenly the cloud cleared, and instead of looking straight out in front and seeing them, apparently looking straight up in the air, there they were towering above you although they were hundreds of miles away.

At 8000 feet it takes a little time, a few days, to get accustomed to the rarefied air but when you do you feel amazingly fit. As I said the officers' mess was some 200 feet or possibly more below the barracks, and the way up was more like a really steep staircase than anything else. We felt very fit and consequently very hungry and found that the mess produced very good porridge and also a thing one never saw down in the plains – cream. For the first few days I started off breakfast with a generous portion of porridge and cream, followed by a good hearty breakfast after that, but soon found out that the 200 feet up this frightful sort of staircase was really too much, and porridge had to come off the menu except on Thursdays, which was a holiday, or Sundays possibly when there'd only be a Church parade much later.

Having climbed up to the barracks we carried out very elementary training. Of course most of the men were only new recruits,

33

who had recently come out from England, so this was quite suitable. There was a good deal of physical training and a little later when they were getting fitter and accustomed to the height, we did quite a lot of long distance running which personally I enjoyed much more than many others. There were a number of quarters for married officers all down the hill round about the mess. Most of these had friends and the wives of men who were still down in the plains staying with them, and there were also quite a number of unattached females staying with friends in Chakhrata. The result was a great many parties, picnics, dances, theatricals, and so on. Rather like Kipling's *Plain Tales from the Hills*, although not quite so dramatic.

Return to Cawnpore

I went down to Cawnpore with a detachment before the hot weather so as to let a few more, who hadn't been particularly fit, come up to the hills. The first day's march down the road to Dehra Dun went all right but in the night, at our first camp, we heard that there had been a landslide a bit farther down the road and it was impassable. It took three days to make a path across the fallen side of the hill and that was only just wide enough to walk in single file and quite useless for bullock transport. We therefore had to take the bullock carts to pieces, which were carried over together with all the baggage and re-assembled on the far side. It was then another two or three days' march down to Dehra Dun. This was a time when I got to know the N.C.O.'s and Jocks very much better and, being with them all the time and being the only officer, saw much more of them than usual and enjoyed it all. A little later down in the plains, when I was made scout officer, I also saw much more of the men. I used to take them out into camp so really got to know them well. With detachments in the hills and most other people on leave, Cawnpore was very quiet, but I did a certain amount of shooting round about, chiefly sand grouse and green pigeon. The green pigeon were really quite good shooting. They used to fly very fast and they had the advantage of being very good to eat. I think it was on one of these shooting expeditions that Pat Hewitt and I found a nice deep pool in an almost dry river bed and decided to bathe. It was really nice and cool and quite large enough for a good swim. Whilst we were doing this an elderly gentleman with a grey beard came along, squatted down beside the pool and watched us with great interest. When we came out he got up looking rather disappointed and as he walked away he said something which we interpreted as meaning 'there's a big crocodile in there'.

We Sail to South Africa

We left Cawnpore in about the middle of December and at Bombay embarked on the *Sudan* – a rather old, small, P. & O. boat which had been made into a trooper: not too uncomfortable, but she could bounce about a bit. And that reminds me of one of my most unpleasant experiences at sea.

On Christmas Day we were approaching the Mozambique Channel between Madagascar and the African Coast. This is a rather shallow channel and in rough weather can be very rough indeed. We had a very cheerful Christmas party. On Boxing Day I should not have been feeling very well in any case, but we ran into this bad weather and were being thrown about all over the place. To add to my discomfort I was orderly officer and one of my duties was to go down into the lowest hold of the ship and supervise the issue of rations. To get down there one had to go through two troop decks where there were a large number of men being violently sick and down in the hold the smell was really appalling. I don't think I have ever had such an unpleasant half-hour in my life.

We arrived at Durban in beautiful weather, everything smooth, bright sunshine and it looked very delightful. All along the quay there were rickshaw boys, one of the means of transport in those days being a rickshaw pulled by a large Zulu wearing more or less fancy dress with a huge horned head-dress and grass skirt with bells and things attached to it.

We were to be stationed at Bloemfontein and at that time it was two days' journey by train. On arrival we had to march out to Tempe where the barracks were, some three or four miles out of the town. We took over our lines from the Argyll and Sutherland Highlanders who, as always, had had a pretty good party before leaving. They'd burnt down a lot of things including the mobilisation store and a variety of other huts. They left a rear party behind to finish the handing over commanded by a Major Sutherland. The second evening we were all sitting in the mess after dinner and an agitated waiter came in to say that the kitchen was on fire. Major Sutherland was so accustomed to this that, without looking up from the paper he was reading, he merely said 'Well, put it out!!'.

Tempe was rather bleak and bare after Cawnpore but we soon settled down and found quite a lot of people there we liked very much. The other infantry battalion was the D.C.L.I. There were also the Carabiniers, a nice, cheerful lot, and a brigade of gunners. Our brigade was commanded by Charlie Townsend, later of Chitral and Kut-el-Amara fame. We were soon issued with the new short Enfield rifle and started training in rapid fire. Other training was based very much on what had been learnt during the South African War, then only, of course, eight years before, as opposed to India where there was always great emphasis on mountain warfare as carried out on the North-West Frontier.

With the 1st Battalion in South Africa

On arrival of the 1st Battalion in South Africa, all the polo playing members of the regiment were, of course, immediately engaged in trying to find ponies, and there was no lack of offers. When a new regiment arrived any number of horsecopers, particularly amongst cavalry and gunners, were ready to sell off anything they didn't want. Fortunately I was a lightweight and able to get a pony suitable to play on, but not much more. It was not until some time later that I managed to buy 'The Duke', a very well-bred and really good polo pony. As he'd been un-nerved I was able to get him within a price I was able to borrow from the polo club.

The battalion's signalling officer had gone home on leave from India, and then had been posted to the 2nd Battalion, so I was put on to learn signalling and become the signalling officer. This suited me very well indeed, because as signalling officer I was entitled to a horse. I also had to learn semaphore and the morse code up to a standard required for passing into Signal School, and consequently I didn't have to attend parades which I didn't want to. In those days company commanders were not mounted and many of them were very annoyed indeed to see a junior subaltern riding about when they went on manoeuvres as they had to walk. I must admit that in certain cases this gave me great satisfaction.

Very wisely we brought our mess cooks with us from India. They were really first-class. The only trouble was that they had to get their normal supplies of opium, but that was arranged, and their value was very soon demonstrated when we went on manoeuvres in Northern Transvaal. They usually managed to get on in advance, and on arrival in any camp or bivouac, before anybody had settled down at all, our cooks had made made their fires out in the open and they were frying sausages and various other things available. The excellent mess sergeant always had a large supply of port available, and so we were always surrounded by hungry visitors from other regiments just coming to see how we were getting on. But as I said before, we were never allowed to indulge in all these luxuries until we were quite sure that all the men were settled in. Sometimes we were in bivouacs sleeping in the open, and sometimes in tents. The nights were very cold and we would wake up in the mornings with little patches of ice where we had been breathing on our pillows.

At the Signal School in Pretoria

My next move was to the School of Signalling at Pretoria, or rather Robert Heights, which was about three or four miles out of Pretoria. The headquarters of the South African Command were at Pretoria, and it was there that I first met Lord Methuen, who was C.-in-C., and Lady Methuen. Lady Methuen, after the Field-Marshal's death, came to live at Asham House, where I now [1969] live with my sister.

The garrison consisted of, I think, a brigade of gunners, the 3rd Hussars, the Hampshire Regiment, always known as the 'Happy Hants' and the South Staffords, known as the 'South Stiffs'. Signalling in those days was almost entirely visual – morse code, flag, helio and 'begbi' lamp. Also there was a primitive field telephone. It was with this that most communication was done, with a morse key. Of course there was also semaphore but that was usually used within the regiment over a short distance. At the beginning of the course we did a great deal of sending and reading morse code with flag, helio and lamp. When reading there was always a tendency to guess at a letter, or sometimes if you thought you hadn't got the right one, and thought you knew the word coming, you might put one in which you thought would be right. It was for this reason that the sergeant-major instructor had a permanent cry of 'Have faith', 'Have faith'. He was cavalry sergeant-major and a very good instructor who had a variety of these sayings.'Have faith' is one I particularly remember, and the other one was 'Ignorance and force never trimmed a lamp'. This was because night signalling was with the 'begbi' lamp; an oil lamp which had to be very carefully trimmed to get a perfect flame and consequently the best results. It had a louvre shutter in front which was actuated by a knob on the top. We constantly repeated his shout around the Signalling School – 'Have faith, have faith'. 'Ignorance and force never trimmed a lamp'.

In South Africa, especially in the Transvaal, with its very clear atmosphere and great deal of sunshine, the heliograph was one of the most important things, and the large heliograph – I think it was the ten inch – I have read over a distance of 90 miles. The field telephone cables were carried on mules – a roll on either side and on the top of the saddle, the telephone. In order to communicate with headquarters, we had to stop, earth the telephone, and then, if lucky, get a verbal message through, though usually we had to use morse key. Then someone had the bright idea that it was not necessary to stop to earth the telephone, but it could be done by attaching the earth wire to the mule's bit, and you would get your earth through the mule. Most mules didn't think this was a good idea at all; they reacted strongly to the series of small shocks through their mouths, and a good deal of cable and various things were lost.

Towards the end of the signalling course, the C.-in-C., Lord Methuen gave us a test. He was at a central point on a high kopje and he sent messages to us to move about in various parts of the countryside. We worked in pairs – an officer and N.C.O., both mounted, and carrying heliographs and flags. The C.-in.C. selected a spot on the map, a message was helioed to one of the groups to go to it and open up as quickly as possible, and off we galloped, set our helios, and got into communication. It was all a great success and apparently the old man enjoyed it very much indeed. I had rather an unfortunate experience however. We'd arrived at a tree which we though was the correct position and, in order to get a better view, I climbed up it. I got about half way up when I saw a large green mamba, one of the most poisonous snakes in South Africa, sliding down the branches towards me. I only had about ten feet to drop, I suppose, but I made the drop very quickly indeed!

This was the year of the Union of South Africa when the Duke of Connaught came out for the proceedings. There were several days of parades, processions, presentations, garden parties and so on, and during this I was appointed galloper to the Brigadier, commanding the troops at Roberts Heights. I enjoyed it all very much except for an unfortunate incident during the big ceremonial parade. The adjutant of the 3rd Hussars very kindly lent me a military saddle, but I had no regimental bridle – black and silver,

South Africa, 1910. The Duke of Connaught, in frock-coat, arriving at Cape Town for the celebrations to mark formation of the Union. On his left Brigadier General 'Charlie' Townsend, followed by Rory Baynes, his galloper.

with black and purple throat ornament – so I went down and borrowed one from James Jack. This was just a trifle big and loose for 'The Duke' but I didn't dare have any more holes bored in Jack's bridle. At all events everything went very well for a couple of days. Then on a big ceremonial parade, during the advance in revue order, with gunners on the right, then 3rd Hussars, then the two infantry regiments, and so on, I was about ten yards behind the brigade commander and to the left of him, with the staff captain ten yards behind and to the right. Suddenly 'The Duke' laid back his ears, and slipped the brow band back over them. All I could do was to lean forward and push it up, during which he turned round once, and then stood again alright. I heard the staff captain angrily growling at me that I'd spoilt the whole parade and felt very unhappy about it. Just as the parade was moving off Lord Methuen, in the uniform of the Colonel of the Scots Guards, rode up to me and I thought: 'Now I am for it; he has come to tell me my army career is finished, I'd better get home at once'. However, what he said was: 'That was a very difficult situation, and you got out of it very well'. There are very few Field Marshals who would have taken the trouble to do that. As a member of the staff I had to attend all sorts of functions and one amusing one was a presentation. It was rather an ordeal for some of the Dutch ladies who had to walk in, make a curtsy first to the Duke, then to the Duchess and finally to Princess Patricia; some of them when they had got through the door into the hall where the presentation was taking place, funked it and tried to break back. We members of the staff, about half a dozen of us, were standing more or less in the slips, we had to catch them and push them back in to line again.

My Return to the U.K. on Leave

I was now due for home leave, but there was no signalling officer to relieve me. So my first job was to get one of the latest joined officers and train him, and then get him off to the Signals School. The lot fell on poor Hopkirk, and I worked him pretty hard. I was also offered the job of assistant commandant at the School of Signalling, but the Colonel wouldn't let me go, and I was much too anxious to go home even if he had consented. I'd done myself pretty well whilst at Pretoria and on visits to Johannesburg and so the next job was to raise all the money I possibly could to go home with: selling ponies, clothes, boots, anything that would fetch a bob or two.

At the Mounted Infantry School, Longmoor

I had six months leave, and as the battalion was due to come
home just at the end of the year (or early in 1912), I didn't want to
go back to South Africa, paying my own passage for such a short
time. I managed to get appointed, as a temporary job, to the Mounted Infantry School at Longmoor, Hampshire. I was a sort of
supernumerary, and at first given the job of remount officer. What
a remount officer had to do I haven't the faintest idea, as I never
did anything about it in particular. We were each of us issued with
a charger, but it was very much a matter of luck as to what sort of
horse you got; that is to say if you hadn't been there before, and
they didn't know you. I was very lucky indeed as I was given
'Lenity' a black Irish mare standing about 14 hands 3 inches.

'Lenity' had recently arrived from Ireland and no one knew anything about her. She was fast and a bold, though inexperienced
jumper. She gave me one toss over each different kind of fence but
after that never made a mistake. She jumped rather too fast for
some people's liking, certainly that of the assistant commandant
who rode her one time. She never showed a sign of refusing and
was particularly good at timber, in fact at times almost too good as
on one occasion I was leaning over to unlatch a gate and she
decided to jump it. Fortunately we managed to remain together. In
the first point-to-point in which I rode her, the Inter-Battalion
Mounted Infantry Race, about half-way round we hit a big grower
in the middle of a cut-and-laid fence, and fell. But later on, in the
second one, I really ought to have won. I was only beaten by half a
head. I left the run-in a bit too late and was coming up fast but just
didn't get past in time. Later in the H.H. (Hampshire Hunt) point-
to-point I entered her in a race open to the Aldershot Command,
with over thirty starters and a lot of thoroughbred horses brought
in from the cavalry at Aldershot. For this I borrowed a heavy hunting saddle, much heavier than the one I always used but in spite of
that I had to carry 7lbs of lead to make up the necessary 12½ stone.
We finished a very good third; a marvellous performance for a
small mare like that against a lot of big horses. Normally the
mounted infantry cobs worked throughout the year, but 'Lenity'
had done so well that she was turned out to grass for the summer.
My second charger was quite a different proposition: 'Orange Pip-
pin', an Argentine cob who was very clever. Instead of galloping on
and standing well away from his fences, like 'Lenity', and flying
them, he went right up to them, stopped dead, and just as you

'Lenity', Rory's brilliant little mare.

The Mounted Infantry School, Longmoor, 1911. The drag hunt point-to-point.

thought that he'd refused, he shot straight up into the air and over. He was as clever as a cat and could change on the top of a post and rails. His was a much slower progress but in spite of that we managed to keep well up with the hounds. We had two drag lines every week, each of which required two horses, and I usually managed one day a week with the foxhounds – the H.H., as the Hampshire Hunt was always known. I was able to do this as I was loaned a big thoroughbred mare. The owner didn't like riding her very much as she took a considerable hold. We got on quite well together when I took to riding her with a snaffle with a Newmarket gag, which one never touched except in an emergency. She again was a very fast bold jumper, standing well back, giving one a wonderful feeling flying over a big fence.

The drag was a spectacle enjoyed by the landowners and farmers. There was one well known line we laid on in a park near a big house and the first jump was quite a wide and deep brook. There was always a large lunch party at the house and therefore many guests waiting to watch the jump; they were always rewarded by quite a fair number of horses and riders going well into the water. In another place a farmer had a well known post and rails, and he used to assemble his friends with lots of spare timber to mend the top rail when it was broken. Once a rail was broken everybody rushed out in front of it, kept the rest of the field back whilst they nailed another one on the top, then got away and let the young gentlemen have a go at it.

At the end of the hunting season I became the scout officer, which again gave me considerable scope. One interesting job I was given was to go out with the scouts and one of the earliest wireless sets. This was carried in a cart and manned by one or two sappers. We were sent about the country, being controlled from headquarters by wireless. We were rung up and told to go from one place to another, and then given instructions to find billets. The police made all the billeting arrangements and did it very well. We had one very pleasant evening in Midhurst, where there was a boxing tournament at which I was asked to referee. In those days the police had no difficulty in suddenly finding stabling for some twenty or so horses in any village or small town. The wireless worked very well up to about twelve miles or so, as long as there were no woods or hills in the way.

At the end of the last course when I was there we were inspected by King George V. We produced a magnificent battle for him, doing all our dismount work, jumping off our horses and so on, and everything went very well and happily until he thought it was about time he went away. We were all assembled for a conference at which he said a few kind words to us and then somebody said: 'Where's the Queen?' – nobody knew! Someone said they thought the school adjutant had taken her away to show some recruits jumping and so people like myself were sent off in all directions to try and find her, galloping through the pine forests and shouting at everybody that we met. It was about half an hour before she was discovered, and I understand the King wasn't very pleased about it.

Rejoining the 1st Battalion in Scotland

By this time the 1st Battalion had returned from South Africa and were stationed at Maryhill. They were out in Barry Camp at Buddon when I went up and rejoined them there. Instead of riding all the time it was walking, and instead of hunting and polo, it was golf and sailing. Those who know the training area no doubt appreciate that you can get plenty of exercise over those sand dunes. We played most golf on the Panmure course, which is just across the railway within a few hundred yards of the camp, and also at Carnoustie. However, as a rule Carnoustie was so crowded that we kept away from it.

When August came, as was the custom in Scotland and I think has always been, all training stopped before the 12th and the regiment returned to Maryhill.

Maryhill Barracks were quite the gloomiest and grimiest in the United Kingdom. There were four high narrow barrack blocks, so narrow that when beds were down there was hardly room to get between them down the middle of the barrack-rooms. It was said that the reason for this was that the sappers who helped to construct them mistook the inside measurements of the rooms for the outside ones and so they were cut down several feet. The officers' mess, on the other hand, was large and spacious, though equally grimy on the outside. There was a large hall then a big ante-room and dining room, all of which were decorated with trophies of the chase. These were of considerable interest to us then.

The mess was well and comfortably furnished, although this suffered sometimes on guest nights. Not so, however, our quarters, which were very much the same as when I first joined the Militia at Bedford. A bare wood floor, bed, table, chair, chest of drawers, looking glass and, I think, some kind of hanging cupboard, a washstand with basin and mirror, and a tin bath. There were also a couple of candlesticks, as although I think there was gas in the mess, there was no such lighting in the quarters.

The Musketry Course at Hythe

Just at this time Pat Hewitt and I went off to the School of Musketry at Hythe for the four-week course; and that was something! I suppose thirty or more regiments were represented on the course and amongst these there were a variety of customs. It seems that some of the Guards customs and behaviour had not been appreciated on previous courses, for in the opening lecture by the Commandant we were told that we were not allowed to throw Guards officers into the canal.

In those days there was no trouble about long hair, but King's Regulations required one not to shave the upper lip, and whiskers, if worn, should be 'of a moderate length'. A short time before there had been a certain amount of trouble as a cavalry subaltern, one Lord Rocksavage, had insisted on shaving his upper lip and growing whiskers and when he was told he was not to do so, he'd resigned rather than change. Eventually he was allowed to go on serving, but this rather broke the rule.

At Hythe on this occasion there was an officer of, I think, the Rifle Brigade, who was clean shaven and he was told that he must grow a moustache. He complied by coming out with a different kind of false moustache each day. One time it was black and waxed at the ends; another red and drooping; on another occasion about four or five little hairs on either side. All these things kept it lively and interesting. There's no doubt it was a very good course and one learnt as much as could be expected at the time about weapon training and so on, and perhaps remembered it later.

I've just remembered one or two more things about the School of Musketry at Hythe. The first and most important is that we were concentrating to a great extent on rapid fire, the short Lee Enfield rifle being introduced 18 months or two years before, and we were trying out all sorts of ways to discover the best way of using it. It was the rapid fire, of course, that was produced by that rifle which was so very important in the very early days of the 1914-18 War. The other was a sartorial change. Up to about that date our service dress jacket had a stand-up collar, but they had just allowed the turned-down collar, which was to be worn with a white collar and a black tie. Some of the individuals thought this a good opportunity to wear a regimental tie with their service dress, and also the designers of the new service dress jacket hadn't laid down anything about what sort of shirt was to be worn with it. I think they assumed that with a white collar people would wear a white shirt. I think many did but we had one splendid example at Hythe – I think he was in the H.L.I. – at any rate he turned up with a bright pink shirt with a beautiful pattern of little black devils with curly tails, carrying pitch-forks, all over it.

I Return to the 1st Battalion in Glasgow

As I was so near home at Ringwould I asked for a fortnight's leave after the course, but as I was going to take part in the play 'All of a Sudden Peggy,' which was being produced in Glasgow and run very largely by Mrs Combe, the C.O.'s wife, I was told that I had to get back to Glasgow and get on with the rehearsals. 'All of a Sudden Peggy' was very successful. We ran for a week in one of the Glasgow theatres and had several outside engagements.

Although the officers' quarters at Maryhill were by no means comfortable, the mess proper really was very good and well furnished, and the messing was excellent. We had a French chef who did us extraordinarily well at the rate of, I think, 3/- a day. In other ways things were well done, too. Both the mess servants and officers' servants had a very smart livery of a blue coat with silver buttons, red waistcoat and so on; all rather expensive, though, I fear.

I used to go to St. Andrews with the MacAllans and stay with them. Both the MacAllan brothers were natives of St. Andrews and scratch golfers, so staying with such well known golfing families I sort of automatically became an honorary, temporary member of the Royal and Ancient, and there met a lot of the best amateur golfers of the time. I also played with some of the well known old professionals like Andrew Kirkaldy and Willy Auchterlonie. Members of the Royal and Ancient were most hospitable, and when I went at any time I was very kindly received.

Eventually I got my spell of leave. On getting home I told father all my difficulties, how expensive life was in serving at home and suggested that perhaps the best thing I could do was to apply to go to the West African Frontier Force where they were very well paid. At that time West Africa was still known as 'the White man's grave' and much to my surprise instead of father saying: 'No, no, my boy, I can't let you go out there; I must increase your allowance', he said: 'I think that's a very good idea'. I put in an application to go to the Frontier Force. Some who went out there, came home after a year or little more on six month's leave and had a very good time on the proceeds.

In due course my posting order arrived. It was to the Sierra Leone battalion of the Royal West African Frontier Force (RWAFF). I started to collect the right kit. At that time, the only means of transport in Sierra Leone was by carriage on men's heads and so everything had to be arranged in 60lb. loads which was the limit one man was expected to carry, on a day's march. There was one other thing – everything had to be packed as far as possible in white ant-proof boxes so they supplied me with some tin uniform cases which are supposed to be airtight as well as being ant-proof, with wooden bottoms, so they wouldn't buckle up when carried on a man's head. Other items of camp equipment were special types of table and chair and most important, a bath – a tin bath which had a lid to it and a wicker lining in which things could be packed, and in this bath load one always carried a lot of clothes and so on. When on trek, on arrival at the destination, the bath was unstrapped, the lid taken off, the basket containing clothing was taken out and then the bath was prepared. Other things had to be arranged as far as possible in those 60lb. loads and so the next people I had to go to were Fortnum and Mason for food, or 'chop' as it was called in West Africa. We took out approximately three months supply of tinned food and these were packed in things called wooden 'chop boxes' which were very valuable not only at that time for carting all one's food about but I used 'chop boxes' for packing things in years and years afterwards. They were very well designed. I can't remember exactly which firm supplied everything but there were such things as mosquito nets, mosquito boots and then a special kind of medicine chest or first-aid box which was made by Burroughs and Welcome, especially for lonely travellers in the tropical jungle.

My next visit was to Cogswell and Harrison for a sporting 303 rifle, and a supply of 12 bore cartridges. It was suggested in those days that it was better to have brass drawn cartridges as they were not liable to swell (the cases) in the damp tropical climate. Fortunately, they weren't as expensive as they are now and I took out a supply of, I think, about 500, all of which were used.

At all events, off I went to Liverpool, where we embarked on an Elder Dempster ship which was not very large. I think she was called the *Abinsi* and I noticed a very considerable difference in her and the previous ships I'd sailed in. The first two had been troop-ships on which there was a certain amount of military discipline and so on. Life, in some ways, was like at home in barracks. Coming home from South Africa, I was in a Castle Line ship, very well appointed for those days and everything was perhaps rather sedate; everybody cheerful and very interested in the forthcoming coronation; that was the beginning of 1911. But the atmosphere in the *Abinsi* seemed to be quite different to the other ships that I'd sailed in. I think it was because, in those days, West Africa, was still called 'the White man's grave' and there was a sort of reckless attitude towards everything. There were the 'old coasters' as they were known as they'd been in West Africa for some time, who took things for granted, knew the sort of risks and so on, and were prepared to take chances and didn't worry about anything very much. There were some of the younger ones going out for the first time who wondered what sort of life it would be and viewed it with some apprehension. There were others rather like us soldiers who were looking forward to change and excitement, the result being that everybody took everything as it came, as I said, a sort of general reckless feeling and that was manifested to a great extent in the evening's amusement which was very largely gambling. The Purser had a roulette board in the smoking room and, in other parts, there were games such as crown and anchor, chemin-de-fer and, in the saloons, probably one or two poker tables. As I said many of the younger ones had no idea what to expect or what they were in for and the 'old coasters' took a delight in telling them horrible stories of life in West Africa and the dreadful things that might happen to them. They recounted some of the more unfortunate diseases such as the filarial worm which would burrow into you and run about inside you appearing one time in an arm and then go up and wander about round your neck and then might go off somewhere else; or tumbo flies which laid eggs inside you, and so on. They took a horrid delight in this! Of course, some of the poor wretches had no idea what it was really going to be like, or what clothes and things they required. There was one poor lad who was going into one of the trading firms, who arrived on board wearing a morning coat and striped trousers which he wore all the way, even when we were in the tropics, as I don't think he had any other clothes at all.

There was one other subaltern on board going to the Sierra Leone battalion with me, who shall be nameless, and his chief interest seemed to be gin. I think that's perhaps why his regiment or his family had encouraged him to go to Africa and keep out of the way. I was rather surprised at this, as in the army generally, nobody thought of drinking gin in those days. The normal thing would possibly be a glass of sherry or port with a slice of cake in the morning, later a little beer perhaps and in the evening, whisky, but gin was practically unknown in those days in a normal officers' mess. I suppose they used to drink it in the Navy as they have done since, but at all events, West Africa was just the place for this young man as then gin was 1s.6d. a bottle, which suited him very well.

The voyage to Freetown took ten days and I quite enjoyed it. On arrival we anchored off Freetown, some distance out. We were immediately surrounded by dugout canoes with small boys shouting for money to be thrown over, and the little devils were extraordinarily clever as they dived after the coins going down collecting them in their mouths. They'd got all sorts of names that they used to call the passengers; one of the favourite for ladies was Mrs Langtry; for men very often Mr Macaulay or possibly Lord Roberts.

West Africa 1913-14

We were taken ashore in small boats and on arrival we were met by an African gentleman who used to see our baggage through customs. I don't know if he worked only for the Frontier Force but, nevertheless, he was very efficient and rejoiced to the name of Tony Lumpkin, which was not surprising, as most of what were then called 'creoles' in Sierra Leone, took these well-known names from writers and stage characters. They were descendants of the freed slaves and not the half-caste kind which were found in the West Indies. At any rate, Tony Lumpkin took charge and saw us through everything very quickly and easily.

The regiment had sent down a couple of orderlies to meet us. The orderlies were, at that time, called soldier servants or, subsequently, batmen and these were two experienced ones, who spoke very good pidgin English and were able to understand the white man's language very well. In Freetown we met a man at the Government Rest House where we stayed who started off by teaching us pidgin English for everything in conection with food. We'd brought out various tins of food from Fortnum and Mason but you then had to learn that anything tinned was called pan chop; for instance, a tin of corned beef would be 'pan beef'. To take pan out of a box or out of the store was called 'pull it' hence 'Pully a pan of chop'. So, if a boy came in and said 'I done make; I pull one pan of sardine' – what he probably meant was that dinner was served and the cook wishes to take a tin of sardines from the store, possibly to make a savoury.

We had to wait some days for the train to take us to Daru as it only ran once a week.

The Sierra Leone railway ran from Freetown on the coast to Pendembu on the frontier between Sierra Leone and French Senegal up in the north; a single track line and the total journey took two days. The first day took one as far as Bo, where the train stopped for the night, and the second day on to Pendembu, but it also stopped at Daru, which was the headquarters of the Sierra Leone Battalion of the West African Frontier Force. I think the reason that trains only ran by day was there was a fear of running into wild animals at night, also I don't think that the railway staff much liked the idea of driving about in darkness because there was no knowing in country like that what sort of devils and strange things were about. The train through to Pendembu only ran once a week. Of course it took four days – two days there and two days back – and always in Africa at that time after any such effort everybody required at least a day's rest. In addition, it fitted in with the weekly mail boat coming in and so our mail arrived up country once a week. At Daru, it was taken off at the railway station. When I was at Bandajuma, our mail was unloaded at Bo and it took a carrier two days to bring it down to Bandajuma, carrying the sack on his head. I don't think there was much traffic besides the mail train once a week; a certain amount of goods traffic, perhaps one train. There were various other stations and passing places, or side tracks, but the mail train was the chief service.

We entrained at Freetown into a not very comfortable carriage by modern standards, but having been in India and South Africa on a variety of trains before, I didn't find it too bad. The carriage was like a small tramcar with cane bottomed seats along each side. There were shutters to keep out some of the dust and smoke from the wood-fired engine and the first coach behind ours was occupied by the orderlies and servants and then there'd be the third-class passengers.

I later discovered that rather than travel in a first-class carriage, it was more comfortable to have a deck chair put up in a luggage van. The springing was not so good but the seat was not nearly so hard. One of our orderlies – 'Blackie Pendumba' – was a seasoned traveller and saw to it that we were made thoroughly comfortable; all our supply of drinks and so on in the coolest possible place and our food supplied.

The first day's journey took us as far as Bo, and on arrival there, we were met by members of a company from the Gold Coast Regiment, who'd been sent there when the trouble with Leopard cannibals was getting serious. The idea was that when the Sierra Leone Battalion had been increased by two or three companies they would return to the Gold Coast. We found them a very cheerful lot and they entertained us magnificently.

The next day's journey took us to Daru, the headquarters of the Sierra Leone Battalion. We had our own platform just below the barracks. Here we found the majority of officers who were stationed there, waiting to greet us, and a fatigue-party dressed in what was the general working uniform of the Frontier Force at that time – khaki shorts, a brown jersey and a pill-box shaped green woolly cap with a blob on the top which was called a 'Kilmarnock'. They were all drawn up and very smart, but the officers were just a little peculiar. Most of them were wearing the most ragged looking shorts, some with khaki shirts, others just wearing a vest and so on; but what was more peculiar was their strange hairstyles. Some were almost shaven bald, others with longish hair; there was an odd beard, whiskers, and moustaches of various shapes and sizes. It wasn't until a little later that we found out what was going on; there was a sort of hair growing competition. All these things gave a little spice to life in these places so far away from home, and without many distractions. They were a very nice and cheerful lot. As I said, most of us that went out there did so because we were people who enjoyed a cheerful life and were thoroughly broke; were going to make the best of things wherever we went; liked excitement and a certain amount of adventure; and having first of all paid off some of our debts, could make some savings with which to go home and start all over again!

Life at Daru

Daru was situated on the banks of the River Moa, which there, I suppose, was quite 200 yards wide, possibly more. It had been built about ten years before I got there, in the Edwardian style. The mess was a long wooden building with a corrugated iron roof, and contained a dining room, an ante-room and a billiard-room, which was always considered a necessary part in those days, of any officers' or sergeants' mess. It had a wide verandah in front, the middle of which protruded, and so made a large open-air room

A view of the camp at Daru.

which was the one chiefly used. At the back, there were kitchens, store rooms and so on. Each of us had a hut in its own grounds. I suppose the hut was 20 feet long by 10 or 15 feet wide, and was built of wood with a palm-thatched roof over the whole thing, carried on a large iron framework, leaving a space about six feet or so between the top of the wooden hut and the palm thatch. The thatch came down all round to about six feet from the ground and this left room for a wide cool verandah all round the centre part of the hut. It was on this verandah that we used to live very largely, we had a camp-bed out and slept there in the afternoon. Altogether a most suitable form of construction for the tropics. There was also an orderly room, consisting of about three offices, built in very much the same style as the mess; a quartermaster's store; an armoury where rifles were kept at night; and an armoury shop. Each company also had a small office built of concrete, with floors of the local laterite.

All this was built on a low hill overlooking the river and lower down along the river bank were the men's lines. These were all mud huts thatched with palm. Each man had a hut to himself and his family. Privates, or 'Frontiers' as we called them, were each allowed one wife in barracks; corporals, two; sergeants, three; and a company sergeant-major and, of course, regimental sergeant-major and so on were allowed as many wives as they liked and their huts could accommodate. But I don't think many had more than two, seldom three on the spot, although they probably had a good many in their own towns. The lines were full of small children called 'piccanins'; chickens; sometimes guinea pigs; an odd dog or so, but in spite of all the population, they were always scrupulously clean. The lines were also along the river bank and the little piccanins – naked creatures with huge fat tummies with a string of beads round them – used to wander about, falling in and climbing out of the river. I never heard of any being drowned and nobody worried about them at all. One also sometimes saw them carrying enormous great knives and other dangerous objects. But again I heard of no accidents. It was considered that any small child could look after itself and I think very often if they were left alone they always would. Of course, the sweeping and cleaning of the barracks was all done by the men's wives and that, no doubt, was one of the advantages of the system, though I can't imagine it working over here. There were other odd customs more of which I shall probably remember as I go on.

One was that the whole garrison fell in at tatoo roll call. Roll call having been called, they then sang 'God save the King' only they used to sing 'God shave our gracious sing' and it was thought that probably they thought it was all in praise of their singing. After that was over the sergeant-major gave the blessing. This was an old Victorian custom which started, I think, when the Frontier Force began and they had a strong missionary influence. We also sometimes had a night alarm. The alarm was sounded and everybody turned out and they usually got on parade in a matter of about two minutes. All they had to have was to be armed and properly equipped, and half of them used to turn out stark naked but for a belt, bandolier, bayonet, machet, rifle and so on. The roll call was then called by the platoon sergeants who had their platoon roll on a piece of board. Of course, they couldn't read but learned it all off by heart; they insisted on having a hurricane lamp to read by, usually holding the board upside-down.

Whoever laid out the barracks had a rather Victorian idea of what the sports requirements were for British officers. Of course, there was the billiard table in the mess; there was also a piano; there was a concrete cricket pitch for a net near the mess, and also, of all things, a 'sticky court'. The sticky court was about the same size as a tennis court, concrete, but with a wooden wall about eight feet high all round it. Sticky was a game played very much like tennis over a net, but you could also take the shots off the side walls, back wall and so on; a mixture between squash and tennis. It was open to the sun and the concrete floor collected heat throughout the day, the wooden walls kept it in and you can't imagine anything much more uncomfortable than playing a game of that kind so near the Equator.

It got dark at six o'clock and the custom then was to go around to one another's bungalows and have a drink or two; then, after an evening bath, to change and assemble in the mess for half to three-quarters of an hour before dinner. During that time we used to play whisky poker and have odd drinks, one of which was much in vogue – a milk cocktail – I didn't care for it very much. It was made of gin, condensed milk and angustura bitters. At all events, this was a very pleasant and cheerful time. We also had a small 'chop' and all these little hors d'oeuvre things which were supplied.

The mess staff consisted of the mess corporal and, I think, two orderlies. The corporal, whose name I forget, was one of the few who could read and write and he was very keen on table decoration. There was a little plant, I don't think I ever knew its name, that produced a little flower rather like a red catkin only longer, and the corporal had managed to write all sorts of things on the table with these flowers in quite clear letters. I always remember on one occasion, a particularly important one, when we came in we found written all round the table in red catkins: 'Ham to-night, gentlemen, if you please'.

There was also a billiard marker in charge of the billiard room whose great thing was translating English into pidgin English, and he had one famous rendering which always pleased visitors. His translation of the end of 'The only way' was well known. It should read: 'This thing I do is a far, far better thing than anything that I've ever done before. It is a far, far better rest I go to than any I have ever known'. Cole translated it as follows: 'This thing I go do he find bad passed all I done; now I go blow good fashion'. Very few of the frontiers could read or write. The orderly sergeant was known as Fatty Palmer – a very fat gentleman and most amusing – had come I think probably from Freetown on the coast. There were a number of nicknames which we used, in some cases we gave them other odd names – 'Blacky', or if lighter skinned 'Borie', which in Mende meant yellow. We often heard a recruit who came from somewhere near a mission station who said his name was 'God' – the idea being that white men like God and therefore he'd be welcome as a recruit. I don't think anybody was really enlisted under such a name as 'God'.

Enlistment and recruit training kept us pretty busy for the next two or three months. I'd always done a good deal of drawing and painting and my brother Keith had got me a complete outfit of sketching materials. At that time photography was very difficult in the tropics owing to the effect of heat on films, and it was almost impossible to develop them out there – they had to be sent home. I spent a lot of time and got a lot of amusement sketching. The first parade was at 6.30-7.00 and all the training was done in the morning. In the afternoon the majority went to sleep until about 4 o'clock when they had tea and turned out for games. But I used to go off either to the bush, or to the railway bridge or to the local villages and sketch. I got most enthusiastic about it and was always longing for the afternoon to start on another picture. I don't think I brought any of these sketches home. Many went to the Acting Governor's wife and her sister who visited Daru on one occasion, and I gave the rest away to other people who wanted them.

I'd been rather disappointed because nobody seemed to take much interest in shooting. We were told there wasn't much to shoot, the bush was so thick that you couldn't see anything and that it was not really worthwhile trying. However, I was determined to have a go and with about two or three others we used to go out on Thursdays, the traditional army holiday, and Sundays. The going was pretty hard, but we went into the rice fields where we shot the occasional bush fowl; francolin, a partridge-like bird; and a certain number of green pigeon; also later, when I'd found out a little more about it, a few guinea-fowl. It meant I started to learn something about the bush – moving about in it and living in it.

At one stage I was lucky enough to shoot a crocodile about twelve feet long. This was a little farther down the river. It was rather interesting, as when I shot him he went down to the bottom of the river in a deep pool and we could see him quite clearly. The crocodile was lying at the bottom of this deep pool and it is very difficult to tell how dead a crocodile is, but I had a man with me who was a member of the crocodile family. There were lots of these families who were sort of affiliated to various animals; there were the crocodile, snake, leopard, bush cow, buffalo and so on families. They were on friendly terms and they felt absolutely safe from any animal which was affiliated to their own family. We immediately cut down some of the creepers, like liana, bashed them about and made them into a 'tie-tie', which was the Sierra Leone equivalent of rope. He then dived in and tied up the crocodile with tie-tie. I don't think the crocodile seemed very pleased to see him, but at all events he managed it alright, hauled him up and there again was a lot of food for those who liked crocodile. I don't think that any members of the crocodile families objected to eating them. All this made certain complications; although a man might belong to a leopard family he would not necessarily be a member of the leopard society which was one of the ones we were trying to suppress which killed children and ate them at a ceremony; a sort of ritual. Besides the leopard society, there was, a little further north, a crocodile society.

Not very long after this we had a tough old gentleman brought in who'd had the inside of his thigh almost bitten off by a well-known crocodile which lived in a river near his village. It used to wait about for people coming down to wash and so on. It got hold of him but he managed to get a machete which he was carrying into its mouth, twist it about and thus got away. He was in a pretty bad way when he came in and we brought him into hospital. At that time I used to help the M.O. with operations and various things and helped with this and stitching it up. In order to make quite sure it was the crocodile who committed the crime and not members of the crocodile society, the inhabitants of the village were determined to catch it. They got a large number of people with big strong sticks. They went into the river, made a circle and advanced shouting and yelling and pushing their sticks into the bottom of the river in front of them until they closed up and had a ring, like a fence, built all round the crocodile. They then threw in nets. These were made of tie-tie which was very strong and they were used for their kind of hunting. They used to cut tracks through the bush, spread the nets out and then beat the game into them – small beef, antelope and so on, and so catch them. At all events, they chucked in a lot of these quite heavy nets on the top of the crocodile so that he was all tangled up; they then went in and tied him up and put him on to a sort of sledge and dragged him in some 20 miles or so to Daru to show us that it was a real crocodile that had done the damage. I went up to tell the victim, who was getting on fairly well in hospital, and the old man burst into shouts of laughter, covered up his head in a blanket, and I left him still laughing heartily.

Mayhew the M.O. asked me to help him with several operations. There was a dresser, with some sort of medical certificate, who gave the anaesthetic and I did the job which I have since learnt might have been called theatre nurse, or theatre sister perhaps; having all the instruments and everything ready, and waiting. This experience in the hospital was really rather useful to me later on when I had to go out with half a company, all their families and everything else, entirely on my own.

Pay-day was once a month and the money, all in West African florins, was drawn from the Treasury at the District Commissioner's headquarters at Kenema, about three days march down the line. Incidentally, Kenema was the place where all the photographs for Gerald Durrell's series on *Catch me a Colobus* were taken. All money out there was called copper. Copper was brought up in .303 ammunition boxes, landed at Daru, where most of the men were paid – but there was another company at a place called Kailahn, right up on the Senegal frontier, and one days march up from Pendembu, which was the end of the railway.

My first job outside H.Q. was to go up to Pendembu with a normal escort of an N.C.O. and four or five frontiers, take the copper up to Kailahn and hand it over to the Company Commander. It was then that I had my first acquaintance with the carriers, the natives who were supplied by the chief of each town, village and so on as required. Each of them was not supposed to carry a load of more than sixty pounds and loads varied very much in weight. Those who didn't really know used to rush for the smallest load which they'd hope would be the lightest. It was at Pendembu that I first saw the rush of the ignorant towards the copper box which was, as I said, an ammunition box filled with florins and although the smallest of the lot was very much the heaviest.

Kailahn was the normal bush station of those days. All mud huts thatched with palm: officers' mess; quarters; company office; all just the same, varying from the troops' quarters only in a matter of size. It was built on a hill which in some ways was an advantage, one obviously got more breeze and it was cooler, but the disadvantage was that it was struck by lightning regularly every year during the tornadoes. Every year one or two huts were struck by lightning and set on fire and this was sometimes a disadvantage and sometimes an advantage. On one occasion, the company office caught it and there was a most interesting scene. The company clerk, a creole from Freetown, rushed into the flames and started getting out all the papers and the Company Commander was immediately seizing them and throwing them back again. There's nothing like a good fire to cover up all sorts of deficiencies and it might cover up everything for a matter of two or three years.

There was a lance corporal in the battalion called Samba Kaita who came from Timbuctoo, and when he went on leave he always started off by train to Pendembu then walked up through Kailahn. As a rule the frontiers had one months leave a year but we had to make some allowances as far as Samba Kaita was concerned, as it took him one month to walk home to Timbuctoo, and another month to walk back. So he was always given, perhaps not a whole three months leave, but very nearly that. Very difficult to fit these things in but nobody else seemed to mind, and Samba Kaita, when he was with the battalion, was a very good lance corporal and one always got a little information about what was going on in French territory and other parts.

Making a New Station at Bandajuma

When we'd recruited up to strength to form a new company, I was sent off with half a company to Bandajuma to clear the bush, lay out a new station and get everything ready. This place was in the middle of what was the leopard cannibal country. I not only had the half company but also their wives and families to go with me and to be looked after, which was really quite an interesting job. To get there we had half a day in the train to a place called Bangbama and then three days march along these narrow bush paths – not more than about two or three feet wide – down to Bandajuma. I was met there by a nice old gentleman with a grey beard, flowing robes, carrying a three thonged whip and some six hundred labourers, who were to do the job. I crossed the river, walked up a hill and found a place more or less where it had been suggested that we should build the barracks. I cut a piece out of a tree by the path, walked on another three hundred yards or so, cut another bit out on the other side and said, 'Now then, just clear the forest either side of that'. In they went and in a very short time they had all the trees cut down and burnt, and a clear space made for the barracks.

It was at this time that some of my medical training from Mayhew was useful. They'd sent me off with a large 'chop box' full of various odds and ends of medicines: some openers, some closers, and so on, and a list of them giving some idea what they might be used for. I had a morning sick parade each day and I managed to get on fairly well.

When the bush was cleared the next thing was to lay out the general plan. This was done as usual with bits of rope made of 'tie-tie'. We pegged out the position of the various huts, stretched out the ropes and then scratched along the ground to show where each hut should be. The layout consisted of about twenty huts for the private soldiers, or frontiers as we called them. Others for corporals, sergeants and one large one for the sergeant-major. As I think I'd said before, the allowance of wives in barracks was one for each frontier, two for a corporal, three for a sergeant and any number for the sergeant-major. Of course the sergeant-major being a wise old man never had more than two about. The general system for acquiring wives, which of course had to be bought with sheep, cows or any other currency, was first to obtain an aged, experienced cook and then, as he went on, the next one would be a more attractive younger one. By the time you were a sergeant-major like Sergeant-Major Brown, you'd have quite a number, and out of them, in barracks, you'd probably have kept the best cook and the most attractive of the later ones. Talking of Sergeant-Major Brown reminds me that he had the Royal Humane Society Medal. The exact details of how he got it I was never quite able to find out but I think a bridge broke and he jumped in some torrent and saved a life or two. But he would never understand that he'd got the medal for saving life. He always called it his swimming medal and thought it was entirely because he was such a good strong swimmer. To get back to the provision for all these wives: there were two large cooking huts for the frontiers' wives, another one for corporals' another for sergeants' wives and of course the sergeant-major had his own kitchen at the back. Everything was just the same: daubed huts with a palm leaf roof. I also had to make an officers' mess and officers' quarters. Each of us had a round mud hut with a thatched roof, and there was a hospital hut, and that was about all of it when we started.

Whilst we were in the middle of construction, the huts having gone up pretty well, the walls being up and we were getting on with the palm thatch, I got a message from the district commissioner asking me to come along and help in raiding a village. The operation was planned by the D.C. and was to be carried out by his assistant with court messengers. These were a sort of local police and I was to meet them and join in the more serious business of preventing the leopard cannibals escaping and rounding them up. The assistant district commissioner would deal with the legal part of the business. It was a very secret operation and I was asked to go out as though on ordinary patrol to another little village. The assistant district commissioner, with his court messengers, would go to another village not very far away, apparently on some other errand. Then, at night we would meet, go off to the suspected village, encircle it just before dawn, move in, round everybody up and search the huts. It all had to be very, very secret, particularly as a number of people from the village we were going to raid were working on the building of the barracks. Also, amongst them was the chief's son. At all events it all worked out fairly well. Berry, incidentally, the assistant district commissioner was a large and horribly fat man. We went to our various villages and then got up in the middle of the night, met at the appointed place and arrived at the village by dawn. We then went in and collected everything we wanted. We had to get some of the inhabitants out from under beds and others who were hiding in the roofs of huts, but we didn't have any particular trouble. We also found quite a number of the strange medicines they used and other queer things too. For instance, a padlock with a lot of string twisted round it which was said to be used for locking the district commissioner up in his office. Apparently by using this and a sort of fan arrangement like little parachutes that you waved round, you then sent the spell from the padlock to the district commissioner and he'd be unable to move out of his office until the spell was taken off. Of course that was most valuable when you were going to have a leopard cannibal feast and didn't want to be interrupted.

We were in the middle of searching the village, dragging people out of hiding and so on, when a strange procession came from a neighbouring village. All the inhabitants were tied together with tie-tie in a long line, being driven by a frontier who was on leave. He was one of the tallest men in the country, over six feet, which was most unusual amongst Mendes, whose average height was no more than five feet four inches. Kiskhama had been on leave in his own village which was fairly close, but being a loyal frontier, and having signed on to serve His Majesty, he'd heard there was a raid on the neighbouring village and thought that the inhabitants of his own village might also be required. So he gathered them all in and tied them altogether with tie-tie. This gives some idea of the astonishing loyalty of the Africans when they'd enlisted and joined what they called 'the work'. Family association didn't matter a bit – they had joined 'the work'.

The operation had been very secret and up to that point successful, but the secrecy which had been managed by the assistant district commissioner – the fat man Berry, had gone too far. It had been arranged that we'd take a certain amount of food and things with us for breakfast in the morning, and Berry's messengers were to go to the villages where we'd left our bedding, etc, and bring them on during the course of the day to the village we had raided. Unfortunately things had been so secret that Berry hadn't told the court messengers where to bring these items. We waited throughout the day for all our home comforts that we should want that night but nothing came. We'd got a certain amount of food – a chicken or two – there were papaw, bananas and things growing so we wern't starving. Fortunately we had a drink or two, but when night came, with no bedding, mosquito nets, dinner, or anything else I spent a most unpleasant night. Some rather torn lace curtains were found in one of the huts and a couple of camp chairs were put side by side, then the curtains were put round us to keep mosquitos out as far as possible though not very effectively. I slept under this, or rather was kept awake under this, as the fat Berry snored appallingly all night. However, fortunately the following morning some of my escort went out, found our loads and servants, and brought everything else in. During the operation, the village chief – I think he was probably a guilty old man – died of heart failure or shock. As I said, some of his people were working on the barracks, amongst them his son. On return to Bandajuma I found the son working at thatching the roof of the hut that I was going to occupy, and so I said to him, 'I am very sorry, I think I killed your Daddy'. He replied, 'That's fine Sir, now I be chief'. After that everybody seemed very happy and that made me relax too. When the barracks were finished the rest of the company came down, commanded by a Captain Bill of the Suffolks. It was then possible for me to go out on patrol.

We used to go out on patrol for a week or ten days at a time with an escort of about six frontiers, moving about the country to show the local inhabitants that the army were present, and they had better not indulge in leopard cannibalism. This, of course, was a great opportunity for shooting, and as soon as possible I went with a patrol down to the south where the bush and forest weren't quite so thick and there was a better chance of doing some big game shooting. Eventually I managed to shoot a 'bush cow', which was the name given to the dwarf West African buffalo. It wasn't really such a dwarf but it was small compared with the enormous East African buffalo. Shooting a bush cow was the height of most big game hunter's ambition at the time. They could be very dangerous and would always charge you when wounded.

I was now very nearly due for leave but, to my consternation and dismay, I was told that before going home I should have to sit for my promotion exam to captain down in Freetown before sailing. I hadn't done any preparation for it and in fact I don't think I'd thought about it. I managed to get hold of the book on the special campaign which candidates had to be examined on. I read that with care, but really made no other preparation at all. I was very busy and enjoyed myself very much and I didn't care about the idea of settling down to studies in the bush. At all events I went down to Freetown for the exam. I suppose thanks to Major Heath's thorough grounding, when I was going up for the Militia Competitive, I'd remembered enough to pass quite comfortably. I was rather amused because in Freetown I met one of our subalterns who'd been on leave and spent a lot of it at an army crammer. He told me that it was quite impossible for me to pass unless I'd done something of the kind myself, but in the result I passed and he did not.

Leave in the U.K.

The voyage home was, as always, a most cheerful affair, everybody looking forward to getting back home. Most of us, having saved a certain amount of money, were determined to spend as much as possible on arrival on every kind of luxury. There were, of course, a lot of sick people on board, which was unfortunate, and it was not unusual to have several people die. In fact you might say an average of one every two days. We used to get up in the morning about six-thirty to seven o'clock – walk about the deck in pyjamas and dressing gowns, usually with a brandy and ginger ale. About this time the engines stopped and everybody went back and looked over the after deck, where the daily funeral was taking place of the unfortunate gentleman who'd died in the night and who was being pushed over the side.

This time, arrival at Plymouth was very different to my earlier arrival at Southampton. The first one I had no money at all but this time I felt positively rich. I took the train for London, and enjoyed what subsequently became a custom on returning from Africa. This was to dine at Scott's starting with a dozen oysters followed by a grilled steak and mushrooms. On the same boat coming home there was a man Crane who I'd originally known at the Mounted Infantry School at Longmoor. He was very anxious to learn to fly and at that time it cost £75 to do the course. I was rather keen to do the same thing and we'd arranged to meet later and, I think, go to Farnborough. At all events life in London and various othere places, especially these good dinners and so on, soon saw through my hard gained capital and when the time came to go flying I hadn't got a spare £75 about me. Crane did do his course but he hadn't completed it when the war started and he, poor lad, went out as an observer in some plane and got shot down very early in the war. I think on the whole I was very lucky to have expended my substance on riotous living rather than going up in a plane.

By now my brother Keith had a studio in London, just off the King's Road, Chelsea and he found rooms for me in a neighbouring square, which I kept throughout my leave until the war started. I spent quite a lot of time in London and had a very cheerful time; the rest of it down at Ringwould with all the old forms of entertainment. I really had a most enjoyable leave, which was brought to an end by the outbreak of the war.

The Declaration of War and Training a New Army

When war was declared I was at Ringwould and either that day or the day after I had a telegram telling me to rejoin the 1st Battalion at Maryhill. When I got there I found intense activity: reservists coming in and all sorts of preparations being made. Also arriving were a lot of officers – veterans of the Boer War – many of whom had just dug out their uniforms, and looked as though they had just arrived from South Africa without having time to wash or change since arrival. I can't remember how long it was but it was two or three days after I got there, and we were really getting things going when Kitchener made the announcement that he required a hundred thousand men, which were to be raised immediately. Robertson was commanding the battalion – always known as 'Blobs' – and he sent for me and told me that he was very sorry, but as I'd been away from the battalion for some time, I must be one of the three officers who had to be sent off immediately to help with this business of raising a new army. It was a bitter disappointment, but there was nothing to be done about it. Off I went to the depot with one Peckham-Corry, who was fat and not very healthy. He was slightly senior to me, and there was also a very newly joined 2nd Lieutenant called Briggs.

At the depot at Hamilton, instead of the intense activity of Maryhill we found utter confusion. Reservists had been coming in and were being fitted out, and the staff were getting on with things fairly well, although the depot was extremely full. But immediately the announcement of the first hundred thousand was made, volunteers started pouring in: their tents were pitched in a sort of playing field in the middle of the barracks, and every available space was taken up by men sleeping. There was not enough preparation in the way of food and rations, and we had to send out into Hamilton and collect everything possible in the way of food. The first night things got so bad and the depot was so full, that we had to close the gates and at intervals open them and then charge the people outside thus keeping them from breaking in. All this first kind were a pretty rough lot, many of whom were unemployed, and they were only too anxious to join up and get some food and pay. After two or three days I was sent off with Briggs, two hundred men and half a dozen or so N.C.O.'s from the depot. We were put on a train but we'd no idea where we were going.

We eventually found ourselves at Bordon. Nobody at Bordon

A group of officers and N.C.O.'s of 9th Scottish Rifles at Bordon Camp in 1914.

knew anything about us either, but I met the garrison adjutant, whom I'd known before when I was in the Mounted Infantry at Longmoor, and he told me that I'd better go and choose some barracks to live in. I chose Martinique barracks which were nearest the station and went in there with my two hundred men. I think the outgoing battalion must have left a rear party who were still cleaning up, because I don't remember having any particular difficulty getting into any of the buildings and I think the mess must have been open, and possibly a cookhouse. I do remember that the officers' quarters were left as though the occupants had been moved when only halfway through their packing. In various places full dress uniforms were lying about on chairs and beds. We got some food somehow, but for the first few days it was like camping in a deserted house, though we must have got organised quite soon. Amongst the N.C.O's who came down there was Sergeant Brown, later Colour-Sergeant Brown, an absolutely first class man who'd been at the depot. He and I decided that some organisation ought to be started and, rather like Captain Mannering of the Home Guard, I appointed myself adjutant and he appointed himself orderly room sergeant, and we settled down to the work of organisation and documentation.

Some days later another two hundred men arrived and these were put into other barrack rooms which we took over. Later came another two hundred, and then some officers of various sorts and kinds. I think the first officers were probably old volunteers dating back to the previous century. There were certainly two ancient majors, and then more odd people turned up. There were those who'd been on jobs in various strange places, odd Indian army people who'd been on leave, and so on. What was interesting was the sort of men who arrived with each party. The first lot that I had taken down were a pretty rough crowd who, as I said, had more or less broken into Hamilton and joined up for food and jobs. The next lot were rather better. They'd had jobs and had given them up and joined the army. Then later a superior class came down. These were all very well dressed, with a couple of them carrying suitcases, and later on came an even smarter variety. Also a lot of ex – N.C.O.'s who were most useful. One thing about it was that with all these men to select from there was no difficulty in finding somebody for any kind of job such as cooks, clerks and people who did all kinds of mending such as boot makers. I also found as mess president a man who was one of the directors of the Savoy Hotel in London. We didn't really know what to call ourselves. We knew we were the Scottish Rifles but which battalion, we were not at all sure and once or twice I think the numbers were changed. Certainly the number of the brigade was changed soon after the brigade was formed. I rather think that the number of the battalion changed with it and we became the 9th. In time the barracks became full, until we'd got just about a thousand. As people kept pouring in we put them into the next-door barracks, and those that were sent there eventually became the 10th Battalion. It is difficult to remember the order in which people arrived, but it was some time before Colonel Northey came down to take over command of the 9th. He'd been commanding the depot, and I think it was before he arrived that we had to start the 10th Battalion, into which I put an ancient volunteer major to command to start with. Colonel Ussher, who'd been commanding the 2nd Battalion a few years before, then came down to take over the 10th, and this poor old man, proudly jumped up when Ussher arrived, saluted and said 'I'm proud to hand over your battalion to you Sir', Ussher just said, 'All right, get out'. That was just the sort of thing he did.

To start with, as I said, we were more or less camping. We had absolutely nothing in the way of uniform or equipment or anything else. In spite of that we started marching quite soon, as one of the first things to do was to get the men as fit as possible. I think that broomsticks, instead of rifles, were the first equipment that we learnt to drill with. Then a certain amount of uniform started to arrive. This was all old full dress uniform from every kind of unit, and you got a most extraordinary selection on parade. You'd see a man for instance in a rifle tunic and tartan trews, wearing a straw hat, next to somebody else in a red coat and some civilian trousers. At all events the men were clothed – in a way. The next stage was khaki and everybody got fitted out, not so very long after. There were no khaki overcoats available and so a supply of civilian coats were sent down. This distribution was most amusing as in those days people wore very heavy overcoats, and senior N.C.O's, sergeant-majors and so on all took the large heavy double-breasted kind with belts. Other junior N.C.O's had double-breasted ones without belts, whilst the rank and file had to make do with the single-breasted ones which were not so handsome.

I can't remember how many hours training we put in per day but the training syllabus came down from the War Office. We had to fit in so many hours on each subject for every company every week, and I had to make out a chart of the times and places of various kinds of training to ensure that we distributed it properly, as well as the training facilities such as ranges, assault courses, parade grounds and so on. These charts were always known by the company commanders as 'my Chinese puzzles'. The first great occasion was when we got a complete battalion on parade, though strangely dressed, and took them out for a route-march as a battalion. By that time we had chargers, so Northey and I were able to ride. We were very pleased on one occasion when we passed the 10th Battalion – still commanded by Ussher – as none of them had any uniforms, and Ussher hadn't got a charger or his uniform yet. He was riding up and down his battalion on a bicycle, wearing a bowler hat. It was then discovered that none of our men had been properly attested, so we were instructed to parade the whole battalion and attest them in bulk. The attestation was read out and as far as I can remember they all shouted 'yes' or 'I do', or whatever the right words were.

Soon after we were properly dressed and had got our rifles we were inspected by Field Marshal Sir Evelyn Wood. All this time we heard news coming back from the Front, and received various instruction as to how to make trenches and so on. The first drawings sent were just a trench hollowed out to the side and we started trying to dig these in the sand at Bordon. The first thing that happened, of course, was that they fell in on us, and we had trouble with one or two men getting buried. It was before they'd learnt all about dugouts in France.

Later we had experts who came back from the Front to lecture to us. There was one lecture I remember particularly by General Fergusson, and I think it was mentioned in Ian Hay's book, *The First 100,000*.

During this earlier time my day used to consist of being out on parade at about six-thirty a.m. to see everything started off properly and also to do a certain amount of instructing, because a lot of the officers were, to say the least of it, out-of-date. Some had probably never been up-to date. We then had a short time for breakfast. I was in the orderly room, or round about the headquarters, until lunch which I had in half an hour. Then back to the orderly room where I remained probably up to nine o'clock in the evening. Finally, I had some supper sent over to my quarters, and then to bed. There was a tremendous amount of documentary work to be done, and I tried to go out visiting training as much as possible. I don't know if I insisted on doing a lot of things myself, or if Northey left things to me, but I really did more than I should have – not from the work point of view – but I did a lot of things which should have been done by my commanding officer. I don't think Northey worried about them much.

We then moved to Bramshott and it was a very proud day when we got the whole battalion on parade, fully armed and with a certain amount of transport and we were able to march out of the barracks at Bordon as a real unit, led by our pipers. I'd started getting some pipers very early in the proceedings and one of the first was boy Gibson from Dunblane who was fourteen years old and afterwards became sergeant-major in the regiment. He was a tough lad who insisted on playing a full set of pipes, although I'd offered to buy him a smaller set, and went out on all marches. He never fell out, but very nearly burst from the amount of food and buns that were given to him at every halt by local inhabitants. He was a most popular person and an enormous help to the battalion. I think eventually we had about six pipers and they really were quite good.

At Bramshott we went into a new hutted camp and here started more advanced training: company training, battalion training, and subsequently brigade training. We were lucky in getting our chargers fairly early on – sometime before we left Bordon – and I was particularly lucky as Northey really couldn't ride. As C.O. he was issued with two chargers – one good steady old horse, a little short of sixteen hands and a very nice lively little mare. I think he only got his leg across her once and then I got her, and she gave me a great deal of enjoyment. On the other hand we found a dreadful old chestnut which could hardly creep along which became Northey's principal charger. Maxwell Henning, who had greeted me many years before in Aldershot, was second-in-command. He brought a hunter of his own, so both he and I were well mounted.

It must have been either January or February 1915, certainly when there'd been a lot of snow, that the division was inspected by Kitchener. We were all drawn up along miles of road at Frensham Ponds on a bitterly cold day. Kitchener was late for some reason, so we were standing about in the snow for over an hour. A good many men were falling out or down. All this time we were training pretty hard, and there was not much time for amusement, but we were now and again able to get up to London at weekends, where we had some very cheerful parties indeed. Of course we were all very keen to get out to France. I shall never forget the shock we'd had earlier after the news of the Battle of the Marne, and then the advance from the Marne to the Aisne. We were all terrified the War would be over before we could get into it.

I was getting more and more proud of the battalion and thought that we'd reached a really good standard when two corporals arrived from the 1st Battalion. One of them was Bill Thomas, the heavy-weight boxer who was afterwards Sergeant-Major Thomas. I was sitting in the orderly room and these two corporals came marching in, halted, turned right, and saluted. I saw immediately that our standard of N.C.O's and everything else was far below what it really should be. It was absolutely amazing the difference between two first-class, smart corporals like that and the rest of the N.C.O's. However, we were now recognisable as a battalion, and for the first time I had the interesting job of drilling the battalion complete. I don't think Northey ever did this.

To France at Last

By about the end of March 1915 we were ready to go overseas, and expected to move almost anytime – the exact date I don't remember – but we eventually went down to Folkestone where we embarked and went over to Calais. Quite a comfortable crossing followed with no incidents.

The only incident was the advance party, commanded by Maxwell Henning. When he got on board the ship he was told that he was O.C. ship. He said – 'I don't mind about that I'm going to obey my instructions'. The instructions were on a his bottle of sea-sick pills. He said 'Here you are, it says take two, lie on your back and look at the ceiling, and that's what I'm going to do'. Anyhow, both the advance party and the battalion in due course arrived at Calais, where we were marched off to a base camp. I shall always remember that first march with a lot of little French boys running alongside shouting 'Tipperary'. After a night at the base camp we entrained to go to Meteren. We detrained at a station some twelve miles away and the battalion marched off, led by Northey. I remained behind to see all the transport detrained, and everything on its way, and then followed on after the battalion, having been shown which way they were to go.

On catching up with the battalion I'd been looking at the map and things didn't look quite right to me. Sure enough, a little further on I found that Northey had taken the wrong road out of the village. I don't know how much further we went, but we arrived several hours late at our destination, where we were met by a somewhat displeased brigadier, who spent an hour or so with Northey!

At Meteren we were in bivouacs, and soon encountered trouble with pigs, through which we lost some of our rations. A part of our rations were tins of bully beef, which men carried in their packs. We were told that the pigs were eating it. Nobody believed it of course to start with, but eventually it was found to be perfectly true. The pigs would chew through the thick canvas pack, through the tin and eat the bully beef. The only other animal we had trouble with in the same way were cows. When the troops had hung out their washing on hedges and various odd places, cows were inclined to eat it. I don't know whether they ate it completely or merely chewed it up a bit but there again, although we didn't believe it to start with, eventually we found that this was also perfectly true.

After a few days at Meteren a certain number of officers and N.C.O's went up to Armentières to join the 1st Battalion in the trenches to get a little experience. We went up with our mule transport and on arrival, the transport was parked in the square, whilst we were all in various estaminets round about having lunch. At that moment the Bosche started to shell the town with shrapnel. I shall never forget the speed with which the transport harnessed up and galloped away down the street to a safer place.

It was most enjoyable meeting the 1st Battalion again, and I spent several days in the trenches learning all the routine and the tricks of the trade. After that the 9th Battalion had arrived at Armentières, and as we were now considered ready to take part in the War we went off to Ham-en-Artois. There was a canal running through Ham-en-Artois, and the troops were able to bathe, so I organised what they called aquatic sports. This was much enjoyed: a variety of races, competitions and so on. When we'd been there about a week we moved up into reserve for an attack. We'd got not far behind the line and went into bivouacs for the night. I had some argument with the farmer, who owned the field that we were bivouacing in, as he wanted to charge us rent, although there was a deafening noise of firing going on within a mile or two away. This was a good start to the battle we were supposed to be going into. However, we moved up closer in reserve, but were not required that day. In the afternoon I'd been exercising the mare on another field. The grass was dry and rather slippery and turning she slipped up sideways and landed on my left leg, giving my ankle quite a nasty sprain. So, instead of going up in reserve to the battle like a normal soldier, I went up riding side-saddle with my knee hooked over my holster and my left foot in a red Moroccan slipper. However, as I said, on that occasion we were not required, and we returned to Meteren where after a few days rest my ankle got reasonably better.

From there we went up into the line, first of all in reserve and then in the front line. At last we were really a part of the army in the field, and no longer Kitchener's army in training.

POST OFFICE TELEGRAPHS.

N.B.—This Form must accompany any inquiry respecting this Telegram.

If the Receiver of an Inland Telegram doubts its accuracy, he may have it repeated on payment of half the amount originally paid for its transmission, any fraction of 1d. less than ½d. being reckoned as ½d.; and if it be found that there was any inaccuracy, the amount paid for repetition will be refunded. Special conditions are applicable to the repetition of Foreign Telegrams.

Office of Origin and Service Instructions.

TO

Regret to inform you that Captain R. M. C. Baynes Royal Scottish Rifles wounded Nr. 16 July. Baynes — further news when received will be wired you fully. Secretary War Office.

Telegram to Baynes's father bringing the sad news that Rory had been wounded on 16 July, 1915.

71

> *During the final stages of the Battle of Festubert,*
> *which began on 15 May 1915, Captain Baynes was*
> *wounded. He was in a dugout when a shell landed*
> *beside it and smashed the lower part of one leg as well*
> *as severely lacerating the other. Back in England the*
> *smashed leg was skilfully put together again and*
> *eventually mended completely, although in old age he*
> *was troubled by ulcers on it. However, as his continu-*
> *ing narrative explains, he could only be passed fit for*
> *light duties for a long time after coming out of hospi-*
> *tal, and it was many months before he could walk*
> *comfortably.*
>
> *It is interesting that he was unwilling to say anyth-*
> *ing about these wounds himself when recording his*
> *reminiscences. Such reticence was part of the creed*
> *which governed officers of his generation and class.*

For the rest of the summer and the autumn of 1915 I was in hospital or on sick leave, and I think it must have been about November when a medical board passed me fit for light duty. I then had
orders to report to the 11th Battalion of the Scottish Rifles at Richmond in Yorkshire. They were some sort of training battalion.

To Training Unit at Catterick

As St Pancras Station, when I was going north to join them, I
saw a rather pompous looking lieutenant-colonel with brass buttons on his service dress jacket – and only one strap to his Sam
Browne – but wearing a Scottish Rifle glengarry with our regimental badge. I approached him and he told me that he was commanding the 11th Battalion which I'd been ordered to join. I
explained who I was, thinking he might be rather pleased to have
anybody who'd been a regular officer, and who'd been adjutant of
a battalion serving in France. However, he told me that he had no
use for me, that there was nothing for me to do, and that if I liked
I'd better have some more leave. I suggested that as I'd been
ordered to report to his battalion I'd better do that to start with, and
then possibly find some other job. At all events I got to Richmond,
and then to Catterick Camp, which was in the course of construction, where the 11th Battalion was stationed. It was soon quite
obvious why he didn't want a regular officer of the regiment about,

or anybody who knew anything about soldiering. I've never seen suh a scruffy lot. They were all doing infantry drill in slow time; all movements with sloped arms, and nothing at all of the Cameronians or the Scottish Rifles. In fact there was nothing remotely soldierly about them. When I discovered I wasn't wanted, I went along to Brigade H.Q. and was posted to a young officers' training unit which was in operation there at the time. This was commanded by a Colonel Bourne, a very nice man, who was an Oxford Professor of Zoology in civilian life. He was a famous rowing man and his two sons were also rowing men, and all of them in their time were in the Oxford 'boat'. I liked him very much and we got on very well together; also he was pleased to see somebody who he knew had had some practical training.

There were some thirty or forty young officers in the company of all sorts and kinds. Some were getting more or less direct commissions; some had actually served overseas; and some had come through the ranks, who had not been in France or elsewhere. They were, all round, a very good lot though varied and discipline wasn't all that good. They were rather off-hand in many cases, and the first job that I was put on to was officer in charge of discipline: a curious appointment which should not have been necessary at any establishment at which normal discipline existed. I was also made mess president, because being the officer in charge of discipline made it easier to control behaviour in the mess.

I started off doing the usual sort of instruction which one gave to the newly joined officer in a battalion, but then suddenly Colonel Bourne told me that I had the gift of imparting knowledge and got me to lecture on a variety of subjects. One which he shot at me one morning was 'banking'. Well, all I knew about banking was how to keep your overdraft going, and in an emergency persuade the manager to let you have a little more. However, I eventually found out I knew a good deal more than any of the young officers and at all events kept them interested. Keeping them interested again was sometime the difficulty. Very often for various forms of training they were in small squads spread out over quite a considerable area, and I discovered that they had a roll-call at early morning parade and then another one at a last parade before lunch. In between some of them managed to slip away into the mess for a quick one, and some spent quite a bit of the morning there. Of course I could not walk very far, certainly not very fast, and was unable to keep control of this, so I put in for a charger. I got a very nice little mare and was able to keep, not only control of the young officers' training, but also managed to have a few days hunting with the Bedale and Zetland.

All this time Catterick Camp was being built and conditions were deplorable. The whole place was a sea of mud; all sorts of buildings were going up; and there were a lot of very rough workmen – probably a lot of them Irish – the sort you always get on these occasions. We had frequent murders, drunks dying in ditches and other similar excitement.

I refused to live in the quarters of this so-called 11th Battalion, and got permission to live in a hotel in Richmond which was really quite comfortable. There I met some people whom I liked very much: some engineers, contractors and various people who were building the camp.

Return to West Africa

I attended regular medical boards, but was always given light duty, and it was not until well into 1916 that I got a change. The Cameroons campaign in Africa had come to an end. The battalions of the West African Frontier Force were going back to their home stations to reform. A lot of the officers who had been with with them in the Cameroons campaign were going home on leave, and some of them returning to their units. Officers with experience in West Africa were wanted to help reform these battalions ready for the next job. I was asked to go back to Sierre Leone as second in command to Bill Hastings, who'd been reforming one of the battalions. He managed to persuade the medical board that, although they wouldn't pass me fit for duty generally, if I went to West Africa's nice warm climate, I shouldn't get my legs and ankles too wet and cold. So, once more I packed up, laid in a stock of food from Fortnum and Mason, collected rifles, guns, cartridges and so on and set off for Africa in an Elder Dempster ship. This was not such a comfortable trip as my last one. We made rendezvous with a convoy in some loch off the West Coast of Scotland and then went out into mid-Atlantic in very very rough weather indeed, before we broke off and made for Africa. We had a six-inch gun on the stern of the ship to shoot at any submarines that might annoy us. We had on board a marine gunner who was in charge of the gun and a gun crew was made up of volunteers from the passengers, of which I was one. Amongst us was a little man in the Colonial Service called Branch. He was very small and known to us all as the 'Twig'. We used to do our gun drill for quite a time every morning. It was interesting and good exercise, but in the process of it everybody had to change round the various jobs and

Sierra Leone. A Guard of Honour formed by the Sierra Leone Battalion of the Royal West African Frontier Force in 1920.

Paramount Chiefs of African tribes gather to watch a presentation of Colours to the Sierra Leone Battalion, 1920. An elegant but somewhat informal pose is struck by Major Baynes at the left of the picture.

positions, one of which was the 'loading'. One of us had to lift the shell and push it into the breech, then another one had to put the charge in after it. Poor 'Twig' had a little trouble with the shell which weighed one hundred pounds, and it wasn't until after two or three days that we discovered that poor little 'Twig' himself did not weigh as much as one hundred pounds, and consequently had some difficulty in lifting it. After this he became an honorary member of the gun crew and we got somebody larger and stronger to do the lifting. It was a particularly bright and cheerful voyage. I think it usually is the way, that when there's a certain amount of danger about, people are more friendly.

Once more I landed at Freetown, and was surprised to find that people there remembered me though I had left about two and a half years before. One was Mr. Lumpkin, the customs house clerk, who took over all my baggage and passed it all through customs and saw it up to the rest house.

I took the train up to Daru, the usual two days journey and got things ready as far as I could for the rest of the battalion who were returning from the Cameroons. It wasn't long before most of the men came back but as I have said a lot of the officers went off on leave, or had gone on leave already and there were a completely new lot coming in.

I went back to Bandajuma to take over command of the company there from one Captain Drake. Drake, always known as the 'cock duck'. He used to complain that his brain was so active that he couldn't sleep at night. His chief claim to fame was his addiction to a horrible cocktail that he liked called 'milk cocktail' which I have described before. He used to mix it in a teapot. It was said of him that just at the end of the Cameroons campaign, when the Germans had been defeated and they were waiting to come away, the 'cock duck' gave a lunch party for some friends on the lines of communication, where he'd been kept the whole time. They arrived for lunch on one day and then started on his milk cocktails; they eventually had lunch at 3.00p.m. in the afternoon of the following day. It may possibly be a little exaggerated, but that was more or less his form. At all events I took over the company from him.

I found in Bandajuma several changes. When I'd left it early in 1914, the officers' mess and our huts which I'd built, were just of mud and palm thatched. On return I found they'd built quite a good officers' mess standing up about six feet high on concrete pillars so as to catch all the available breezes. It did catch them all and somethimes during the tornado season it caught rather stronger breezes than one liked. It had two rooms, pantries, wash-

RORY MALCOLM STUART BAYNES

up rooms and so on, a wide verandah all round and was really very pleasant. They'd also built three officers' bunaglows of the same type and design as we had at Daru, they were very good and comfortable and spaced well apart so there was plenty of room to put a large fence round each of them and give each its own garden. In barracks they had also built a tin roofed company office with a store, a concrete armoury where all rifles were stored and locked up at night, and also a concrete rice store. When you're feeding a company of one hundred men or more it is very necessary to buy rice during the plentiful season at a reasonable price. Of course, besides the hundred or so soldiers there were one hundred, or possibly one hundred and twenty, wives and a couple of hundred 'piccanins' (children) to be fed.

It took a little time to get the company up to the standard of smartness, discipline and so on that I liked, and it was rather different to what they'd been accustomed to with 'cock duck'. After all, I had until comparatively recently been adjutant of a very efficient Scottish battalion, and my ideas were rather different. We soon settled down to normal training and routine. From then on I had quite a lot of time, as always in these wild places, to indulge in my own interests, which were shooting and fishing and I could also do quite a lot of reading. As it got dark at 6.00p.m., unless one had been out shooting or fishing as one did sometimes in the evening, one got back to the mess and had a few drinks. After dinner I would put in a lot of time reading.

Before 1914 one of my principal interests out there had been shooting, and I now had quite a useful armoury: two 12-bore shotguns and a double-barrelled 450/400 rifle made for me by Cogswell and Harrison. It had a specially designed safety catch, which you had to put on and did not go on automatically directly you loaded and closed the breech. There had been cases of people being charged by buffalo and animals of that kind, who'd reloaded and then forgotten to take the safety catch off. It was very much better to be able to reload and fire immediately without having to think about anything else. I also had a .303 sporting rifle; a .22 high powered rifle – very effective with a considerable killing power; also a BSA air gun; and a .450 Webley Fosbury revolver – a long barrelled target pistol which could be used with small shot. Looking back on it, I wish I'd had a really good camera instead of so many guns but of course at that time the difficulty was getting films developed. It was very, very difficult to do it out in the bush. One of the problems was getting cool enough water. In sending films home you were up against heat, damp and so on, and it was all very ineffective, but I'd much rather have had some photographs that I could have kept rather than the various heads and so on that were once up in the summer-house at Hill House. I will get on to shooting stories later, but at this time I began to take more interest in fishing.

I took a trout rod out and a certain amount of tackle, and started off in the Wanje at Bandajuma. I caught some small things but in the meantime I'd started reading about fishing in Africa, in any books I could get on the subject. I knew, and had heard, that there were some big fish in the river, so I sent to Hardy's and got a very heavy spinning rod and all sorts of heavy tackle, and settled down to fish for the big ones. Of course, as well as the rod I had to get a big spinning reel and the one I got was a Silex. Having got the tackle the things that I had then to look for were boats or canoes. The only way of fishing in those tropical rivers was by boat or canoe as the 'bush' came right down to the banks. In many cases the trees overhung the whole width of the river and monkeys used to jump from one side to the other. I hope it will become clearer when I tell you some more.

[Alas, there were no more stories to come. Not long after dictating this last instalment of his memoirs, Sir Rory's sister died. He moved then to live with his son in Lake Vyrnwy Hotel, where his son had just become joint owner with a partner. He lived very happily there for nearly seven years, before dying after a short illness two weeks before his ninety-third birthday.]

Joseph Brotherton Maclean

2nd Lieutenant Joseph B. Maclean, 7th Cameronians, 1915.

Joseph Brotherton Maclean

1889   Born in Glasgow, 30 March, the younger surviving son of Hugh Maclean and Isabella Macleod Brotherton Maclean. Educated initially at Shawlands Academy.

1897   Father died.

1902   Mother died. With his elder brother Alexander (b. 1887) taken into the household of an uncle, Malcolm Maclean, who sent the boys to Glasgow High School.

1905   On leaving school, awarded the Sir James Lumsden gold medal as outstanding student 'in the highest commercial class in the High School of Glasgow'. Went to work for the Scottish Temperance Life Assurance Company (since 1951, the Scottish Mutual Assurance Society).

1909   Fellow, Faculty of Actuaries. In this year his brother also became a Fellow and emigrated to America, joining the Home Life Insurance Company in New York City, and (in 1916) the Massachusetts Mutual Life Insurance Company in Springfield, Massachusetts.

1911   Fellow, Institute of Actuaries. Emigrated to America, joining the Mutual Life Insurance Company in New York City. Fellow, Actuarial Society of America, 1913.

1914   Shortly after the outbreak of war in Europe, resigned from the Mutual Life, returned to Scotland (sailing from New York on 28 October) and enlisted in Glasgow with The Cameronians (Scottish Rifles).

1915-17   Commissioned 2nd Lieutenant, January 1915. Gazetted to the 7th (Territorial) Battalion. Assigned to instructional duties, specializing in signals, in the U.K. and Ireland. A/Lieut., 1 June, 1916; T/Lieut., 6th Battalion, 10 November, 1916.

1917-18　　To France, 20 May, 1917. Posted to 1st Battalion, 28 May; joined D company, 2 June. In reserve at Croisilles, 23 June; in action at Lombartzyde, August. Thereafter with 1st Battalion in Ypres area; served at Passchendaele, Meteren, Ypres Canal, St. Quentin Canal, Troisvilles, Vendegies Wood, Forest of Mormal. O.C. B company, from 28 May, 1918. A/Captain, from 27 August, 1918.

　　　　　　　Married Marjorie Maclean in Paris, 19 June, 1918.

　　　　　　　Awarded Military Cross for gallantry in action, Vendegies Wood, 23-24 October, 1918. Decoration conferred in 1919 on board HMS Renown, in New York harbour, by the then Prince of Wales.

1919　　Returned to his position with the Mutual Life in New York City. Assistant Actuary, 1920. Lecturing on actuarial science at Columbia University, 1920-25.

1924　　Published *Life Insurance* (McGraw-Hill). The book was subsequently revised through nine editions and translated into Spanish and Japanese. Associate Actuary, 1926.

1941　　Vice President and Actuary, Mutual Life.

1942-44　　President, Actuarial Society of America.

1947　　Retired to Yarmouthport, Massachusetts; continued writing and consulting work.

1956　　Elected Vice-President, Faculty of Actuaries.

1970　　Died in Yarmouthport, 29 July.

Introduction

From November 1914 until early 1919, Joseph Brotherton Maclean regularly wrote from Scotland, and from France and Flanders, to his brother Alex in New York City. Of this correspondence, however, apart from xerox copies of five autograph pages written in 1915-1916 (on notepaper of the 7th Battalion, The Cameronians), only 86 letters recording Maclean's experiences with the 1st Battalion of that regiment from May 1917 until the end of the war have survived, in typescript. Presumably transcribed by Alex, and passed to his brother after the war, these letters eventually came into the possession of the present editor. There can be no doubt that Joseph also wrote often to Marjorie Maclean (they were married in June of 1918), and recurrently to friends in Scotland and America; but all of that correspondence has disappeared.

The letters reproduced here represent about three-quarters of the 1917-1918 originals. It is the editor's hope that the thrust and force of Maclean's narrative may have been somewhat enhanced by these cuts (in the first instance dictated by limitations of space), since a number of repetitive elements have been eliminated. Otherwise, the letters appear substantially in their original form. Place names, forbidden by the military censor, are supplied for each letter, together with brief explanations of a few military terms. Linking passages have been inserted so that readers may follow the sequence of 1st Battalion operations. Notes for the most part identify persons to whom more than glancing reference is made: regulars and Territorials, actuarial associates, friends and relations on both sides of the Atlantic. Since the autograph fragments bear only marginally on Maclean's account of his experiences with the 1st Battalion, they are omitted here.

To turn from the assured, engaging, and quietly amused air of Sir Rory Baines's memoir, a regular officer's recollection of service to the Crown in peace and war, to the Territorial's relatively abrupt and rough-cast notes from the Western Front is, perhaps, to recall Shakespeare's Armado: 'The words of Mercury are harsh after the songs of Apollo'. In that light, Maclean's letters may easily be undervalued. While they convey a good deal of interesting information about life in the trenches, they were, after all, subject to censorship. Never subsequently revised to bring into focus the 1st Battalion's role in the plans of higher formations, they are not 'military history' in any larger historical sense. Nor are these letters a consciously literary undertaking, imaginatively crafted for artistic or socio-political effect, in the fashion of Edmund Blunden, Robert Graves, or Siegfried Sassoon. Given Maclean's clear enjoyment of Dickens, Butler, Conan Doyle, Thomas Hardy, and of poets too, the letters are remarkably barren of literary 'style'. To be sure, the Scot's pawky wit is pretty regularly in evidence, often echoing the expressive language of the men in Maclean's platoon. Shakespearean and Scriptural turns of phrase now and again sound faintly in his prose. Efforts to render fully the experience of men at war in a world of 'slush and slaughter' recurrently bring dramatic fire to the story. More usually, as the narrative reflects Maclean's gloomy disgust with the literal 'filth' of trench life and its numbing dominance in soldiers' lives, his writing can become tired and slack. Good things are 'A1', bad things 'rotten'; to come back from leave is, more often than not, to return 'with a dull thud'.

Yet the clichés do not really detract from, or much affect, the true value of these letters to a brother. For there is a steady undersong running through them. In the round, they record the responses of an intelligent and decent Scottish civilian (albeit with American overtones) to the unexpected and fearful challenge of war to everything Maclean had been brought up and trained to believe in: to his humanity, at last. They record too a stalwart determination to preserve his balance, and his belief in human values; to 'keep on keeping on' in the face of every kind of pressure. Quiet fortitude, in fact, may well be what gives these letters their particular interest and quality. They remind us of the real thing, the right stuff, beneath the plain-spoken record of events. If the narrative seems now and again simply to plod along, that is in a sense decorous enough for this account of men who go about their duties with steady, laborious persistence. If these letters do not for the most part recall Emerson's 'Man thinking', they evoke an image more immediately to the point: Everyman enduring.

A Maclean family group, Glasgow, c.1902-3. The kilted boy seated at the left of the second row is Joseph B. Maclean; his brother Alex stands at the far right of the back row. Marjorie, Joseph's future bride, stands in the centre, between her grandparents, Donald Maclean and Anne McColl Maclean. The boy in the sailor suit is Marjorie's brother Allan, killed at Gallipoli in April, 1915.

    A few words about Maclean's background and upbringing are in order here. The family had its roots in the Hebrides. Joseph's paternal grandfather, Donald Maclean, was born in 1820 on the Isle of Lewis; subsequently he moved to Glasgow, where he set up in the iron trade, specializing in ornamental railings. The business was in due course carried on by his son, Hugh Maclean, father to Alex and Joseph. Their mother, descended from the MacLeods of Lewis, was the daughter of a Lowland Scot, Joseph Brotherton. Thus the boys derived from their ancestry (to adopt John Baynes's general distinction) both the 'romantic and emotional' elements of highland character and the 'dour and unyielding aspect' of the lowlander [*Soldiers of Scotland* (London, 1988), p.7]. While the move by each branch of the family to Glasgow indicated, in some quarters, a rise in social status (Joseph's mother was distressed that her son should prefer football to cricket), the family was and remained emphatically middle class – for Baynes the class, of six he singles out in British society before 1914, which 'had the fewest connections with the career of arms' [*Morale: A Study of Men and Courage* (2nd edition, London, 1987), p.11].

The brothers' boyhood was not cheerless – both recalled summer holidays in Stornoway with enduring pleasure – yet their memories of that time were pervasively sombre. Joseph was nine years old when his father died, after years of arthritic suffering in a wheelchair; five years later his mother was gone too. The orphans were taken into the household of their uncle Malcolm, a Glasgow oil merchant, with five children of his own. Kindness and brotherly duty extended to the enrollment of Alex and Joseph at Glasgow High School in the fall of 1902, but it was made clear that on leaving school they must fend for themselves. The house at 15, Prince's Street, Strathbungo, was not a happy one for the new arrivals. In their first home the boys had been schooled to recognize the value of discipline and hard work; but every aspect of life in their new abode was directed and dominated by a severely restrictive Presbyterianism that gave force to the familiar text: 'If ye love me, keep my commandments' [John xiv: 15]. The brothers were, of course, expected to take the pledge of abstention from spirits. On Sundays, as Joseph would recall years afterward, 'you went to church in the morning and again in the evening'; for the rest, 'you could go for a walk'. He conceived an intense dislike for the minister, whom he remembered as self-satisfied and arrogant; the boy's resentment sounds again in his sharp contempt for padres and chaplains during the war. Chiefly, the newcomers found themselves treated by their cousins as poor relations, below the salt; regularly reminded in many small ways of their inferior station in that household.

In these circumstances the brothers' best qualities came to the fore. Both were clever and industrious, both mathematically inclined; well-equipped to enter upon an actuarial career. Alex, by nature affable, gregarious, socially at ease, when the time came to break away advanced rapidly in his profession, first in Glasgow, then (from 1909) in America, where his brother joined him two years later. Joseph's character, marked by a certain intellectual rigour and an insistent moral rectitude, was relatively reserved and thoughtful. Dominant in his make-up was an unflinching sense of duty: to his Scottish lineage, to Scotland, to his profession and (in time) his family- and always to his own potential. He could share Alex's enjoyment of Burns's poetry, but preferred Sir Walter Scott, notably 'The Lay of the Last Minstrel' (in particular the opening stanzas of the sixth canto). The more brilliant of the brothers, he had at the age of 24 become, remarkably, a Fellow by examination of the three actuarial bodies of the English-speaking world, with every prospect of a successful career in America. But when war came in 1914 he knew where his first duty lay. Alex had married the American Amy Hodgson earlier that year; in the spring of 1917, a physical disability prevented his effort to enlist with the Canadian armed forces. Subsequently he became an American citizen. Joseph remained a British subject all his life. Still single at the outbreak of the war, and assured that his position with the Mutual Life would be held open for his return, he left New York in October, returned to Scotland, enlisted in The Cameronians, and served with that regiment for the duration of the war.

While the letters tell their own story directly enough, several elements in their pattern are of particular interest. A deep-rooted and determined commitment to exacting professional standards is steadily in evidence, reflecting the Scot's high regard for hard work, especially for work well done, and a matching impatience with slovenly performance; in fact there are two kinds of professionalism here. Andrew Webster's fine obituary for the Faculty of Actuaries observes that Maclean's career was 'interrupted' by his war service. But that is only a partial truth. The letters show that Maclean simply will not permit the war to bring his actuarial career to a halt for the duration. On leave, he visits relatives in Scotland, but also actuarial associates and friends in Glasgow and London. From the front, he corresponds regularly with professional colleagues in America. Alex keeps him supplied with reading matter; he is surprised that his brother prefers 'the heavy stuff', but the younger man, looking on to the resumption of his career after the war, recognizes the need to keep up with developments in his field. While many of his fellow-officers welcome Alex's parcels of comic or illustrated magazines, Maclean is evidently grateful chiefly for articles that bear on his profession. And while Major Ritichie is clearly 'a fine chap', that he is 'a director of the London Life . . . and quite an authority on life insurance' establishes his true quality.

At the same time, to be an officer in wartime is to recognize and embody a disciplined professionalism of another and more immediately demanding kind. Before coming to France, Maclean had developed some proficiency in the signaller's art; for a time he half-expects to become battalion signals officer but when that falls through, he is not unduly cast down. Soon after joining the 1st Battalion he writes, 'I want to get some experience and get out of the greenhorn class, and I feel pretty confident I'll be all right'. 'A short life and a gay one', perhaps; more to the point, the 1st Cameronians 'is a splendid battalion . . . discipline is very strict, but that won't bother me. All the senior officers will be regulars and I'll see a bit of the Army'. What matters is to find out what soldiership means, and to meet its exacting demands: chiefly, no doubt, to build up and maintain the morale of one's men, and so to sustain battalion morale as well.

By nature Maclean is characteristically alert and attentive to details of every sort, actively curious about places and people in and out of the line. 'Everything is intensely interesting.' Of course his first care must be for the men of No. 13 platoon, and his vigilant attention to detail contributes enormously to his success in that regard. After a month with the platoon, he thinks them 'a good lot', whom he is 'getting to know pretty well now'. His pride in his men already speaks through the comment in the same letter on their capacity for hard work to some good purpose, with its implication of a developing rapport between the men and their officer. Thereafter the platoon's accomplishments, idiosyncrasies and character are often noted, with amusement or admiration, but always with a quiet satisfaction in the men's morale. While the small triumph at the A.R.A. competition in February of 1918 takes place out of the line, the platoon's success against Divisional rivals effectively confirms the quality of their officer's 'efforts to foster esprit de platoon', anticipating his steady leadership at Meteren and in Vendegies Wood.

It matters also to fit in with one's fellow-officers, to take part in battalion society, as one can. With Territorials that is not hard; the native-born Scot who went to America, then came home to enlist, must in any case have excited the curiosity of his fellows. He plays bridge with Miller and the newly-decorated Preston, rides with Martin, keeps holiday company with the Canadian Transport Officer, 'a very hard case ... but he seems to like me all right'. Nicol, 'a congenial soul', something of a man for all seasons, perhaps, is regularly at hand, until he is brought down at the Selle. These and other companions presumably appreciated Maclean's active and enquiring mind, as well as his ironic wit, so much to Scottish taste. His natural bent inclines him especially to the company of two professionals already established in civilian life: William Craig, mathematics master of Hutcheson's Grammar School, and Herbert Cole, first violinist in the Scottish Orchestra. Cole was a graduate of Glasgow High School, to be sure, but his mastery in the realm of music – an art that deeply moved Maclean's imagination all his life – gave him distinctive stature in his friend's eyes. Maclean notices the deaths of many companions in the letters, but Cole's death at Meteren is a hard blow: he was 'one of the finest fellows I ever knew'.

To take the measure of regular officers is another matter. At first Maclean is uneasy: they 'simply tolerate us damned territorials ... nothing we do is right to some people'. Further, 'the Sandhurst brigade seems to collect all the medals'. But Captain McLellan's efficiency makes an impression; thereafter, Maclean gradually achieves a frank and cheerful recognition of the regulars' professionalism – and their humanity too, embodied for him by James Jack. Jack may be an eccentric in some ways, 'but he is hot stuff all the same, and as brave as a lion'. It is striking that in his final letter to Alex, Maclean writes as a regular might. 'We're getting the troops polished up and looking like peacetime soldiers again. I have some chance to get a decent company now'. Yet he remains his own man, between two worlds. Americans 'are all right, although they have different ideas from us on some things'. The familiarity of American officers' servants can be disturbing, but a certain ambivalence colours Maclean's reaction: 'If one of ours did that he would be dragged out and shot forthwith, unless the officer dropped dead from the shock'. 'We' are firmly and finally British, but in Maclean's philosophy there is room for Americans too.

The tension between fear and courage, finally, is especially arresting, although this does not fully surface before the return from leave in September, 1917. Through the summer months, war seems often to be an exciting, if strenuous, game. Occasional glimpses of its savage truth can 'put the wind up', yet Maclean's version of even the 'first real scrap' is pretty light-hearted. Life can often become 'a series of explosions', but that's all part of the great adventure. With the return to the front line, however, in cold and rain, the tone changes abruptly. He sees war feelingly now, discovering in its danger, monotony, and especially its 'filth', 'the acme of human misery'. Certainly 'no one but a lunatic enjoys a life like this'. More than once he questions his own courage. After one trying experience, 'on such occasions one is afraid – the bravest man on earth would be'. After all, 'life in the line on a "push front" is simply hell; no one denies that'. But the resilience of his character holds firm. In an emergency, he muses, 'perhaps I wouldn't absolutely "beat it"'. Depression about the war and one's part in it is tempered by the 'good times . . . and if I come through it all safely, it will be a great experience to look back on'. And then there are always the men, for whom Maclean feels affection and admiration: 'the British Tommy is a good cheery chap who can stick a deuce of a lot'. One must do one's best for him. That resolve may well account as much as anything else for Maclean's recovery from the darkness of late 1917.

Thenceforth the letters reflect primarily a stoical capacity to endure. Training specialists at Christmas time, with Nicol, keeps one's spirits up; the A.R.A. success in February is a great thing.

Reading becomes a steadily more important resource. By May, *Barrack Room Ballads* keeps company with *The Oxford Book of English Verse* in his pack. Hardy and Dickens are enjoyable, and Conan Doyle best of all, especially *Brigadier Gerard* (also James Jack's favourite). One learns, though, the special value of a bath, hot food and a clean bed. In early April, 'I'm developing into an old soldier'. Padres and chaplains never convince; what takes their place, it seems, is *luck*. The term recurs with increasing frequency after the New Year, especially from 12 March, when a welcome summons to a ciphering course cancels the 'joyful task' of leading a fighting patrol. From then on Maclean often acknowledges the strange power of luck: hospitalized before the Kemmel Beek fiasco, and again before the disaster at 'Gloucester Road', he once more survives when, just five days before the Armistice, his respirator turns aside the bullet – and preserves it for a thankful Captain Maclean, who remarks, with typical restraint, 'It was sufficiently exciting'.

And yet luck is not everything. Nor are the final letters cynical or morose. Months before, Maclean felt that if life in the front line is unpleasant, yet its sounds and sights are often 'great'. Now, in October, he still records 'new experiences of war' with much of the early zest, even relish. The spirited youth who embarked for the war in October of 1914 has not been altogether transformed. The third pip, after all, has come through at last (with its pay and allowances, duly noted here). A Military Cross is in prospect too. The Brigade has done good work; everyone in the 1st Battalion is in great form. Even the weather has cleared up. Leave to Spain beckons, and across the Atlantic a new life is waiting. Rather touchingly, the strait-laced Scot who could barely bring himself in earlier letters to spell out an oath ('this d--- war' must suffice) at length, on 10 November, employs an Americanism to sum up the experience: 'We certainly had a helluva time'. But the conclusion of this same letter tells a larger truth: 'Exciting times these are; but we do live . . .'

Hugh Maclean.

Letters from France and Flanders, 1917-1918

[When Lieut. Maclean came to France in May, 1917, the 1st Battalion, The Cameronians (Scottish Rifles), had for six weeks played a leading role in a series of punishing efforts to break into the Hindenburg Line between Croisilles and the river Scarpe. Casualties were heavy in these operations, which culminated with the battalion's unsuccessful attack up the Sensée Valley on 27 May. The unit's War Diary for that date, noting that the battalion had made three attacks in ten days, remarks sadly, 'Although the men went well, there was no doubt they were apathetic'. Arriving just after these trials, Maclean for a time regards war chiefly as an exciting adventure. By the end of August, however, he has learned that war can be 'very unpleasant'.]

20th Infantry Base Depot (Étaples)
Army P.O. 517, B.E.F.
20 May, 1917

Dear Alex,

I arrived, with Nicol[1], at above address last night, after a very interesting journey from London. We came by the daily leave train and boat and got to Boulogne about 4 p.m. After reporting and looking after kit, etc., we had about two hours on hand and had a good look round the town, which is quite an interesting place just now. I was airing my French in great form and getting away with it too. We had dinner at the (more or less) 'Grand Hotel du Louvre', but a bottle of wine was the best part of it, and thereafter got on the train again. We had third class carriages (10th class they would be in England) marked 'Officers', and ultimately arrived at address as above. I shall probably be here only for a few days before being buzzed off up the line, but while here I'm not resting – Oh no!

Weather here is very warm, and six officers (and kit) in one tent is a little bit of hades, especially when it is time to get up and wash, etc.

I think you might address letters to Uncle Rod[2] until I know my unit, although letters sent here should reach me.

Regards to you and Amy.

Your affectionate brother,
J.B. Maclean.

20th I.B.D., Army P.O. 517
26 May, 1917

Having had time to look around for a bit, I thought I would write you at a little more length and let you know (as far as I'm allowed) what is happening. Today I have no real work to do but have been employed fitting out, etc. At the Q.M. stores I got my steel helmet, gas helmet, box respirator, first field dressing, iodine tube and iron ration. The latter looks like a horse's feed bag but contains bully [beef] and biscuit, tea and sugar, and is only for use in emergency. This afternoon I had nothing to do but in the evening I got my respirator tested in lachrymatory gas. Tomorrow (Sunday) we do nothing, so Nicol and I are going to visit a small town near here which is a good place, I hear.

On Monday we shall probably be in the 'Bull-Ring' (i.e., training camp) all day and from all accounts it is a H of a place, especially the bayonet assault course, which is gone over under adverse conditions, to say the least of it.[3] The usual time spent here is three or four days to a week, but occasionally longer, depending on the demand. I believe the procedure is to go up to railhead and thereafter get motor transport as far as possible, and then hoof it the rest.

Today I bought a new valise and a pair of trench boots (i.e., knee boots) at the Ordnance Depot, where certain things are sold at cost, and I also got my 'advance pay book' from the field cashier. Of course everything here is in francs and it is a bit of a shock to see how they go, although things are really not dear; but when expressed in francs they seem so.

The weather is infernally hot, and it will be no joke when we get on the move, but I'm quite keen to get up the line and see the place a bit, although I'll probably be a considerable sight more anxious to get down again. Officers and men come and go here every day, some on the way up and others conducting drafts, etc., and all over it is an intensely interesting place, and I'm quite enjoying it in spite of heat and overcrowding.

20th I.B.D., Army P.O. 517
28 May, 1917

I received your letter from Pittsburgh last night and I hope you had a pleasant trip, and impressed the agents with your wisdom.

My posting has come through today and after I leave here, which is pretty sure to happen this week, my address is '1st Cameronians B.E.F.'. That is the regulars all right and I should see a bit there. I hear it is a splendid battalion although discipline is very strict, but that won't bother me. All the senior officers will be regulars so I'll see a bit of the army. Kerr was with them and got in two attacks in a month or so, so it looks lively; but I don't mind, the principle being 'a short life and a gay one'.

Today I was up at the training ground or 'Bull-Ring' from 8 a.m. to 5 p.m. It is a huge place and many thousands of men are put through it every day. Our work today was all in connection with gas helmets and box respirators, and such like. The instructor (a major) said there was one joke always made in connection with gas, and this was it: after a gas attack there are only two kinds of people left, viz., the quick and the dead, and the former were damned quick, i.e., in getting their respirators on. Very cheering! We go up there every day until we are buzzed off and we wear full fighting kit – tin hat included – and I can tell you it's no joke with the temperature as it was today, especially walking on such sandy ground. Well, I'll let you know when I get kicked out . . . .

20th Inf. Base
30 May, 1917

Nicol and I have just got our orders and are leaving for railhead tomorrow morning at 7:50 to join our unit. I think I told you my new address, but, in case not, repeat it: '1st Cameronians'. We should have a very interesting day tomorrow, as of course we are getting nearer the line the whole time.

Today we had a bad time in the bull-ring. In the morning we were twice over their famous 'final assault course' in full equip-ment. It is a series of rushes from trench to trench, the intervening

The assault course, Étaples, 'Bull-Ring'.

Bayonet training, Étaples 'Bull-Ring'.

space being strewn with barbed wire, trip wires, shell holes, etc., and they have fellows throwing huge fir-cones at you all the time to represent bombs. [4] It is somewhat exciting. By the way, the following may amuse you. A lot of men here 'chew gum' and whenever they are caught at it in working hours the punishment is to double-time (in full rig-out) up to the top of a hill beside here. The hill is now known as 'Mount Spearmint'. One of the jokes made by the bombing officer yesterday was: When you see a man sprinting round the trench towards you, don't stop and ask, 'What is it, Bill?' Beat him by ten yards round the traverse and say, 'What was it, Bill?' Another (in a strong Aberdonian accent, he being a Black Watch officer), 'If this hits ye, ye'll have an awfu' bother picking yourself together at the Resurrection'. Very cheerful work as a preliminary to stepping over the precipice . . . .

Div. Depot Bn. [St. Pol]
1 June, 1917

I have come another stage on my journey and am now more than half way from the base to the firing line, and within hearing distance of the war. We have been told that very probably the reinforcement officers will go up tomorrow, so I may be with my battalion tomorrow night, the remainder of the journey being by motor transport.

We had a very interesting journey from the base, being fortunate to secure accommodation in a first-class carriage (excessively filthy) in a train about 500 yards long which crawled all the way. I did not mind that as there was plenty of interest to see on the way, and time did not hang heavily. We passed through the town where G.H.Q. is situated [Montreuil], and further on we saw a large number of 'tanks' – not in action, of course, but some of them in motion. About noon we arrived at the small town near which this depot is situated and were received by the R.T.O. (Railway Transport Officer) who took charge of our baggage and put us on the road to the depot. We had to walk in full kit, carrying every blessed thing, and in a hot sun, and were very tired when we got up here. The road past here runs directly to the front line and last night we saw a long stream of London motor buses carrying troops down to rest camps. Everything is intensely interesting here and we are beginning to feel that we are at the front.

Last night Nicol and I had a good dinner at the Officers' Club here and did some shopping. It is great sport buying things in French shops where they don't speak English, especially things such as a refill for an electric torch – that takes some describing if you don't know what it's called.

Weather is A1. Today we have been working in shirt-sleeves.

[Bailleulval, 6mi. SW of Arras]
3 June, 1917

I have now completed the final stage of the journey from the base, and have joined up with the battalion.

Yesterday afternoon we got orders to move and I was put in charge of all the drafts for the 19th Brigade, but as the divisional drafts were all going together as far as railhead, there was another officer in charge of the train so I had very little to do. Our train left at 7:30p.m. and took just five hours to do the 15 or 20 miles we had to go, but we had a comfortable journey, with only three officers to a compartment. As each officer has to keep his kit with him, however, this is not quite so good as it looks. We had a good supply of eatables and a bottle of port, so we were all right. It was a very interesting journey as practically all that section has been retaken from the Germans, and the signs of war became more evident as we went along: first, old lines of trenches and remains of wire entanglements, then an occasional house with the roof off, or side blown out or burnt down, and so on until ruins became the rule rather than otherwise.

We arrived at railhead after midnight, the only intimation of the fact being that it seemed a more than usually prolonged stop, and finally we realized that we were there. At first there was no one to be seen, but to my relief guides from the battalion arrived just as we were thinking of spending the night in the train. I got rid of all the drafts but our own and found that we had four or five kilometres to march to the village where the battalion was. As we went along we could see the flash of the guns every few seconds, also star shells and other sudden lights showing where the front line lay -about 10 miles off – and the whole time there was the constant rumble of artillery. We got to battalion by about 3 a.m., and again found everything dark and not a soul taking the least interest in us, so we had to hunt out the orderly room staff and get the men into billets.

The village is a fair-sized one, but there is another battalion in it and also an advanced dressing station and one or two small units, and as a good few of the houses are shopsoiled (with shells) you can imagine what kind of billets the men have. After that we were taken to our own billet, which was in quite a decent farm house,

Nicol and I having a room between us (unfurnished, of course). It is reasonably clean and we consider ourselves in luck. When we arrived we got one of the few pleasant surprises we have had so far, as we found that our valises, which we had left behind at railhead, had in the meatime been brought up by the battalion transport; so instead of sleeping in our clothes on the floor we had the luxury of pyjamas, a sleeping bag, and a blanket, and I can tell you it wasn't long before I hit the hay, as I was dog tired. I woke at 9:30 this morning and had to hustle to get round to report to the adjutant. I was posted to D company, and on going round to my company headquarters got an A1 breakfast, including two eggs. At lunch we had salmon and crab, so we do pretty well, and as each company messes separately it makes quite a nice little party.

My company commander is a regular captain – an old 1st Cameronian, and a bit of a nut.[5] He has been very decent to me so far, but I hear he sometimes is the other thing. This village is in pretty good condition and has not been directly shelled, but a good many [houses] are damaged, and there are other signs of past trouble, such as placards on houses, 'Cellar 20 men'. There are also notices to the civilian population (such as it is) regarding action for poison gas, and all the soldiers carry their gas helmets at all times as we are quite near enough to get a smell of it. Of course the place is practically all taken over by the Army, but there are a few civilians, including one old woman in our billet with whom I attempt conversation – not very successfully so far but I'm getting on. We also have one of the official interpreters in our company mess, and I may get a chance to talk French at him.

The Division is only a day or two out of the line and we expect to be out for three weeks, so I'm all right for that time anyway. It doesn't mean, however, that we do nothing, as 'resting' here means training like the dickens. I was asked if I had any special qualifications, and mentioned signalling, but I'm afraid that as I have no experience of that out here I won't get a signalling job, although the fact that the signalling officer was killed in the last attack may have some bearing. The Cameronians were in four attacks last month and had a hot time, and I expect will again.

Weather here is simply perfect and has been ever since I came over, which is very lucky, as it makes a big difference to us. I have had no letters from anyone for about a week now, but I expect to get a big budget shortly and hope I'll hear from you then.

Two Commanding Officers, 1st Cameronians. From left, Major (later Brigadier-General) J.G. Chaplin; Lieutenant-Colonel (later Major-General) P.R. Robertson, D.S.O.

Captain Harry Becher, elder brother of Captain (later Brigadier-General) R.F.R. Becher; Captain (later Brigadier-General) James L. Jack, D.S.O.

[Bailleulval]
10 June, 1917

I am having a pretty fair time here although training is pretty hard. We do all parades in 'fighting order', i.e., everything except pack, and as the weather has been very warm it gets pretty tiring. Yesterday we had a very good trench scheme up in the line which was held a few months ago, including consolidating a position, and I learned a good lot. The ground up there is a mass of wire and shell holes, and there are isolated graves all over the place, some British and some German. This afternoon Nicol and I are going over to the old German trenches about 8 kilos from here and I expect we'll get a few souvenirs, as they were occupied in March of this year. Yesterday we went to see Major Smith at the M.G. Corps, which is located two villages from here. The first of these was in the line and has been very badly knocked about. The church, for instance, is lying in ruins all over the churchyard and there are trenches and dugouts right in the streets.

At present our parades last from 6:30 a.m. to 7:15 p.m. which gives you an idea of what 'resting' is here, but of course we'll long for these good old days when we get back into the line, as I expect we will in a couple of weeks or so. Life in billets is quite all right. We have a band every night – our pipe band one night, and the fifes and drums of the other (regular) battalion[6] on the other, and both are A1.

We have four officers in D company now, and another is coming back from hospital this week, so I expect I'll not have quite so much to do. The regular officers here are a pretty snobbish lot, and simply tolerate us damned territorials; but we get on all right none the less. Our second-in-command got the D.S.O. a few days ago. He is a very nice chap and I imagine a very good soldier.[7] My O.C. company is a bit of a lad; he has been in the West African Frontier Force, and also in a tank, but he considers us canaille, which doesn't help to add to the gaiety of nations.

[Bailleulval]
15 June, 1917

I was glad to receive a letter from you and to see that all goes well. I also got a copy of 'Puck' [an American comic weekly]. If you could send some other (better) paper occasionally it would be appreciated, as we are very short of reading matter now.

We have just got word today that we leave here on Monday as

this Brigade is relieving another in the trenches, so by the time you get this I shall have had my 'baptism of fire', to speak melo-dramatically. I hear we shall be in support the first four days, and then alternate in and out each four days until the Brigade comes out. If this weather continues we shall have a tiring journey up, loaded with all the stuff we have to carry, and even that is no joke. I'm glad we're going. I want to get some experience, and get out of the greenhorn class; and I feel pretty confident I'll be all right. We have heard some hefty strafes [heavy shelling] on our section the last few days and I don't know what sort of time we'll get, but it's the same for everybody.

I feel in A1 form – never better, in fact. There hasn't been any-thing special going on – just hard work, but I've been learning a lot and getting to know the people here. I had a bath tonight, the receptacle being half of a beer-barrel; but the water was hot and I'm clean now, so everybody's pleased.

[Moyenville, 6 mi. SE of Bailleulval]
19 June, 1917

We left billets yesterday morning at 6:30 and bivouacked last night at a 'village' (so to speak) near the line, where we shall remain today; at night we are moving up into the support trenches. The march yesterday was pretty bad, as it was another scorcher of a day, and we were pretty well all in by the time we arrived here. If you have seen Bairnsfather's[8] picture, 'We are staying at a farm', you will understand me when I say we are staying at a village; only his farm would be as good as the best house in this village. Of course we are very close up to the trenches now and we can see occasional bursts of German shrapnel. Yesterday a Bosche aeroplane flew over us and was shelled by the anti-aircraft guns, with the result that we were getting some of the stray bits. One frag-ment landed a few yards from me, and it is distinctly unpleasant to hear the whizz and not be quite sure where the bang is going to take place.

Last night it rained very heavily and no doubt the trenches will be pretty muddy. The ones we are going into have been shelled a lot recently and I understand there are only improvised dug-outs in them. You say that it must be quite different coming out now that we are pretty well top dogs, but there are some considerations which make it worse in other ways. Formerly our troops sat for months in more or less perfect trenches, and some of them hardly ever went over the top; but now that we are so much on the offensive there is a lot more of that sort of thing and the trenches we occupy are very often captured Bosche ones which have been smashed to blazes. You really can have no conception what it's like without being here. Last night I stood for quite a while watching the sky in the direction of the line, and it was a sight, lit up by flashes, some like a big lightning flash, and the lights which are used to light up 'No Man's Land'. I don't know how the enemy stands the continual stream of stuff we dump on him, but it must be hell for him. Of course we get it too, but not as bad as he does . . . .

> *[In the evening of 19 June the 1st Battalion moved up to the support trenches and sunken road behind Croisilles, in preparation for an attack on 'Tunnel Trench' which was duly carried out, to quote the regimental historian, 'by a weak composite company consisting of two platoons of "A" Company and one platoon of "C" Company'. But the attack 'made little headway' and was abandoned at dawn the following day. One officer and six men were killed, two officers and thirty-two men wounded.]*

[Croisilles]
24 June, 1917

I received your postcard from Montreal and I'm glad you were declined for military service. No doubt you are glad to have it off your conscience.

I have now been in the reserve trenches since Tuesday, but expect to quit tonight. The battalion did a stunt last night: namely, a raid on the Bosche trenches, but unfortunately (or fortunately, whichever you like) I was not in it. A and B companies did the attack with C in support and D in reserve. We had one officer killed and two wounded. If we do go out tonight my first visit to the line will have been a very cushy [soft, easy] one, but D company will be for it next time. The stunt started at midnight last night and I was out watching the barrage and the ensuing exhibition of fireworks (alarm signals, etc.) from the German trenches. It was worth seeing. Of course it was too dark to see the dirty work (and too far also) but there was plenty of that. Nicol was not in the show either, as he is in C company and they weren't required.

Weather here has been cold and wet for a couple of days and it's pretty miserable under these conditions, but I am hoping to sleep like a Christian with my clothes off tomorrow night, and I won't half be glad either.

> *[At the end of June, 33 Division was assigned to Third Army Reserve and moved to the area of Airaines, between Abbeville and Amiens, for training. The 1st Battalion moved by way of Monchy-au-Bois, Leal- villers, Naours, and Bouchon to Condé, where it remained until 31 July.]*

[Monchy-au-Bois]
1 July, 1917

We are now on trek for another part of the line but for a couple of days are halted, the reason, I think, being to wait for some of the other units. The place we are halted at is a large pile of stones which used to form houses, and we are encamped in bivouacs. We just about reached the high water mark of misery on Friday night and Saturday morning, but today things are better. We got in about 9 p.m. after a very tiring march in full order, and found awaiting us a field and a large quantity of corrugated iron with which to con- struct shelters, and it was 11 p.m. before we got something to eat. The weather was very cold and windy, and the shelters were any- thing but wind-proof so we were not exactly comfortable. However, the worst was still to come; next morning the rain started to come down like Old Harry and we were just about washed out. We were put to work on some trenches here and very soon were in a most lovely state of filth and altogether felt unhappy. In the afternoon the rain stopped and it is dry today but very blowy, and our bivouac threatens to depart at any moment. Thank heaven we start off again tomorrow.

This is an extremely interesting part of the country. The place we were working in yesterday used to be 'No Man's Land' and I wish you saw some of the shell-holes – about 25 or 30 feet across. There are plenty of dud shells also lying about, some very large ones, and little wooden crosses here and there. Some of these graves have the occupant's rifle and bayonet lying on the top; they nearly all are 'Soldat francais inconnu'. About 100 yards from where I am now are about six English graves with crosses erected by the Germans,

Letter-writing in the trenches.
Captain (later Lieutenant-Colonel) H.H. Lee, D.S.O.

Captain Thomas R. McLellan, O.C. 'B' Company when Joseph Maclean joined the
1st Battalion in 1917.

and inscriptions in German. In the village many of the direction signs are German ones, such as 'Feldweg nach –' [Field-path to –], and, in fact, one of the pieces of wood forming our house is the lid of a box marked 'Granaten'. This village is in a small wood, and every tree is more or less broken up, many of them riddled with bullet holes. I believe the German line used to run through the village; there are old trenches all over the place . . . .

We have a fine strong battalion now and it looks Al on the march. We have a very good pipe band, and altogether it is more like soldiering. I have a decent-sized platoon of my own and am getting to know the men pretty well now. They are a good lot. Yesterday they were the first platoon to finish the task (every one gets the same length to do and can go when it's finished), and were quite pleased with themselves.

Yesterday I had a letter and a parcel from Uncle Rod. He is very decent that way; I am glad when I can make an occasional contribution of eatables to the company mess, since of course we can't get very much variety in the ordinary way. We do very well, however, and this morning they managed ham and eggs, but where the eggs came from Heaven knows. I have the whole of today free as I am not detailed for church parade, and I am going for a prowl round some of the old German trenches with Nicol and Miller to look for souvenirs, although with so many troops about there won't be much left. There are plenty of German 'stick grenades' and entrenching tools and other bulky things, but these are too large and heavy to cart about as our baggage is strictly limited.

I'm afraid I'm a bit late to wish you many happy returns of your birthday; I meant to have mentioned it in my last letter, but I do so now and hope you'll have many o' them. I was very glad to get the papers you sent. Captain Hay[9] (our 2nd i/c company) is quite keen on American comic papers. If you could send some of those pictorial Saturday and Sunday editions they would be much appreciated.

[Naours]
3 July, 1917

We are in the midst of our trek, and although we only get our daily destination we have a good idea of the district, at least, where we are going, and expect then to have a week or two's rest, and then at it again somewhere else. In the past few days we have passed through 14 villages, so I am seeing France at any rate, although the first half of these were the ruined variety, with no civilians or shops, and nothing but devastation and signs of war. Now we have come to a part which is pretty civilised, so that we see whole houses again, and some civilian population. Last night our halting place was a fair-sized village, and I got a clean, if not luxurious, billet in a small house. We started off again at seven this morning, which meant rising at 4.30 as everything we use, such as dishes, etc., has to be cleaned, packed, and carried to the transport wagons about half-an-hour before we start. The day was excessively hot and I can't remember when I felt a march more. It is not the distance that bothers, but the weight one has to carry, which soon begins to tell on the shoulders. This place could almost be called a town, and is the biggest place we have been in for weeks. Our company mess is in a very nice house with a fine garden, and I am sleeping on the drawing room floor tonight, easily the best place I've slept in for some time. The men are all in big barns and are pretty well off. They think anything with a roof on it is a fine billet.

The battalion looks A1 on the march now, as we are pretty strong and have a good pipe band, and all the men are well equipped, and all look the same right down the column. Our C.O.[10] is on leave just now; the second-in-command – Maj. Hyde-Smith, D.S.O. – is in charge. He is a fine chap, and just got his decoration recently. The battalion has also got two more M.C.'s for the fighting in April. I have practically no chance of ever getting anything like that unless I did something marvellous, as I am not one of the Sandhurst brigade . . . nothing we do is right to some people. We have six in our company mess now, as the interpreter, M. Givois, is back from leave; also Martin. Captain McLellan will be back in a day or two and we shall then be at full strength as regards officers. I am quite glad as the more of us there are, the less work for each of us.

[Condé]
9 July, 1917

I have yours of June 5th and 15th. Re yours of the 15th, I agree that the Germans must be pretty far through, and now that Russia has 'come again' and given them un unexpected dull thud they must be about disgusted.[11] Of course everyone is feeling the effects of a long war. There is plenty of 'war-weariness' evident on our side too, but no intention of giving up, whereas the German nation must be convinced by now that they are in a losing fight. The last lot of prisoners I saw were a very poor-looking crowd – thin and small and some very young – but there are bags of the other kind still, and in fact the average Bosche seems to be a very well set up fellow. Yet most of them are sick of it, much more than we are.

We are settled down for a 'rest' in a fairly good village. It is well back from the line and billets are consequently better. I have a small room in a cottage which is quite O.K., and has a bed in it. The window opens on to a very pretty little garden. Altogether the place is quite picturesque. We work from 7 a.m. to noon, and have the afternoon free except for swimming parades in the river (some river it is) [the Somme]. I took that parade yesterday and had a fine swim myself. We have fitted up a spring-board and the men have a great time. Yesterday I had to go to the next town to draw money to pay the battalion from the field cashier. It is 8 kilos (5 miles) from here and when I got there, per cycle, I found he wasn't coming until the afternoon, so I had to go back again then. I met some of the 5th [Cameronians] there who stood me my afternoon tea in their mess, and I got back about 6, to find I was locked out of my billet; but I got in later. I had 15,000 francs with me, which is enough to carry about. That is quite a good little town; but we are within reach of two much larger [Amiens, Abbeville], and I expect to visit them before we leave here. We got a big draft last week with seven officers, of whom two have come to D company; so we are pretty well supplied at present.

We had a pretty stiff march coming here; on the move about five days. On two of those we started off at 5.30 a.m. (reveille at 3.30) so as to escape the heat of the day, and finished up in some small village about 1 or 2 p.m. The billeting party goes on ahead, so that we simply walk into billets on arrival. I have now been in over 30 French towns and villages – some slightly the worse for wear – all very interesting. At one place the lady in our billet volunteered to cook our dinner, and she gave us one that would make the Clarendon [a new York City hotel favoured by English visitors] look like 10 cents. It included wine, red and white, and cognac with the coffee. The people are very friendly; in this case the lady's only son was in the French army, which accounted for her love for us. There are a good many French soldiers in this area; I also saw some of our own Indian troops.

Yours of the 18th June was duly received a short time ago, as well as two papers, for which I am obliged. There is not much in the way of reading matter available here, and any contributions go the round of the company. You ask if I saw Bannatyne or Denham while in Glasgow. I saw the former, and he was asking for you. Both he and Bowie are 'exempted' as indispensable; McNaught (recently married) is also there. W. Ross, Jr. it seems was conscripted some time ago and is in France with Garrison Artillery.[12] I did not go to the C. of G. [City of Glasgow Life Assurance Company] as I had not a great deal of time, and spent most of that getting things I needed.

We are still in rest billets and expect to be here two weeks yet. We have a fine full battalion now, and should be able to do something when the time comes. Weather is exceedingly hot still . . . Yesterday, 14th July, was the French 'Fête Nationale', or anniversary of the taking of the Bastille; we celebrated it in D company mess by getting a French dinner from Givois, the interpreter (or as we call him the interrupter). He got a lady friend to do the cooking, and it was some dinner. The drinks were red and white wine, and a liqueur called 'cointreau'. We certainly enjoyed it.

[Condé]
21 July, 1917

I am glad to hear that you and Amy are enjoying Springfield so much and manage to get around a good deal. That is certainly lovely country in summertime.

I am still out 'at rest' but expect to have just one week more, and then off by train to the business end. The battalion is in great shape now. The Colonel is back from leave, and we know he's here, as he is très moutarde. When he barks out 'Cameronians!' at the head of the battalion the earth trembles and is silent – and we are too, you bet. He is a good man, a D.S.O., and that's the right sort. I think I told you that I'm now company bombing officer, and as White [13] is now off to a signalling school my chances of getting that job are zero, which seems a bit off after all the time I've put in at it. Captain McLellan (O.C., D company) is a great lad for bombing; today we were chucking live stuff all over the place. By the way, I heard that one of the 5th S.R. (White)[14], who was an instructor at the Scottish Command Bombing School, has been sent to America to teach the ways of the Mills Grenade No. 5 and such like. I could have done with that job.

Another job I have now is company mess president, and it is no sinecure, as McLellan is very particular about what he eats and expects A1 meals wherever we are. It will be worse when we get on the move again as we have to forage as we go along. In our present mess the old lady of the house pinches our spoons, and invites her friends in to drink our liqueurs, so she needs to be watched.

Weather here has been very bad all week but it's better today. I was out for a ride this evening with Martin, and on the way home we had a gallop across a big meadow. In the middle of it one of my stirrup leathers came right off and I went flying. I rolled over about three times. It was rather exciting but I was none the worse. That is the first decent ride I've had since I came out here. On Wednesday we had the divisional horse show, the chief patron being General Sir Julian Byng. There was a good display of jumping; one of our officers got second prize, although there were Scots Greys officers there too.[15]

I heard today that Cam Chisholm is missing.[16] There are 19 of the Northants officers missing, and I think it is very likely he is a prisoner. I hope so anyway, as he had gone through a lot, having been twice wounded and got the M.C. People at home think the M.C. is easily got, but the ordinary infantry officer has to do something thrilling before he gets even a recommendation. I'm not thinking about anything like that; all I want is to get out with a whole skin.

YMCA Officers' Rest Room [Amiens]
27 July, 1917

I came here with Nicol this afternoon and am just waiting for the train back at midnight, in a YMCA hut. This is a large town and we had an A1 dinner – some feed, but probably our last for some time, as we fully expect to set off for the big push in a couple of days. We have had fully three weeks out and it is a cinch that we shall get it 'en plein cul' for a while now – at least, all the old hands take that view so I am looking forward to some of the real thing. We are certainly shifting all right, as we got all our new maps yesterday. It will be a two-day train journey, and I'll have a bit of a job arranging the feeding of D company officers for the trip, but I suppose it will be done somehow.

I got yours of the 7th today and also postcards from Amy, from Lenox, a place I well remember, having driven there with Mrs. Adams of Stockbridge.[17] I see you are having hot weather, and so are we, today being a regular 'New Yorker', humid and hot – and it can be hot in this country.

[On 31 July the 1st Battalion entrained for Dunkerque, marching from that town on 1 August to the divisional concentration area near Nieuport. A coastal attack, to be followed by an advance to the Dutch border, had been planned

*for the Division; but this was cancelled when
British attacks on the Ypres front failed. The 1st
Battalion took over a section of the Nieuport
defences, at Lombartzyde, on 15 August].*

[Bray Dunes, E of Dunkerque]
2 August, 1917

I have received your letter of July 13th with photos and other enclosures. At the moment we are having a stiff time – not with bullets and bayonets but with moving in bad weather. We left our rest billets on Wednesday afternoon, marched 7 miles, and entrained. We were in the train until 5.30 a.m. next morning when we suddenly found we had to get out – no time for breakfast – into teeming rain. A couple of miles or so of marching in a downpour and then to barges on a canal for two hours. There was no shelter at all, and everybody was absolutely soaked through. I don't believe a coat exists that will keep one dry under such conditions, and I can tell you 'Miserable Starkey' [i.e. a wretched ragamuffin] had nothing on us. There was also the added knowledge that when we arrived there would be no food and no dry clothes as the transport was coming behind. We got off the barges about 11 a.m. and marched about 2 miles up here on the dunes and sat down to wait for food, which we got about 2. We are now in corps reserve and liable to be shunted off to any old spot at a moment's notice, but at present we are all right in huts which at least have a roof on them. My troubles as mess president have been numerous, but, except yesterday morning when things were impossible I managed to feed our company officers somehow, and today we had the good old ham and egg breakfast. Just now our meat ration is all tinned stuff – 'Maconochie' [meat-and-vegetable stew] and bully beef – and it isn't easy making interesting meals out of that, but I have a good cook and caterer who help a lot.

We are back in the business area all right now; yesterday scores of ambulances passed us on the road. It doesn't add to the small amount of cheerfulness we had just then to see, for instance, a French soldier with his head in a dirty, wet, and bloody bandage looking out at us from one of the Red Cross motors; but of course he is one of the lucky ones. I fully expect to be in the fray in a few days, and our company will certainly get any dirty jobs going, as we weren't in the last 'do'. Weather continues cold and wet, more like February than August . . . .

[Coxyde]
15 August, 1917

We got short notice to quit last night – upwards – and left this morning at 5 a.m. We had reveille at 2.30. At such times one wishes with great fervidness that there were no war. We have come half-way up to the lines and are at the moment occupying French army huts. I hear, however, that we move up to the reserve line tomorrow night, and then carry on progressively, with about six days in the front line. This is a very bad part, water being the predominating element; I believe it is more breastworks than trenches. It is also bad in other ways. The battalion we took over from had ten officer casualties in one six-day tour. The surroundings remind one that there is a war on. Across the road from us there is one of the frequent British cemeteries, and today when I went over to have a look round there were eight corpses lying on stretchers, awaiting burial. The top part is covered with sacking, or a waterproof sheet, but the feet are sticking out, which makes it evident they didn't die in bed. It's a gruesome sight. There are a great many graves of men from Glasgow battalions, chiefly 15th, 16th, and 17th Highland Light Infantry – in one case, a trench with about twenty of the 16th H.L.I. all together.[18] Next door, so to speak, there's a barbed wire enclosure marked 'Advanced Prisoners of War Cage', but today it is unoccupied.

For the moment we are comparatively comfortable and have quite a decent little mess hut for the company. I had a good meal ready within an hour of arrival – and got a vote of confidence from the officers. Fortunately we got a big parcel from Cooper & Co. [a London fruiterer and greengrocer] (not a gift, but ordered beforehand, of course), and it came in handy for the move. The weather has improved somewhat, though we hd some rain on the way up; all last week we had a dickens of a time with the rain, and our huts (Belgian ones) were letting it in badly. However, as one of our chaps says when things go wrong, 'C'est la guerre, c'est la guerre! Triste affaire, malheureuse, malheureuse!' (imitating the old French ladies). Honestly, it is a rotten war. Some of the things one sees here make one want to choke the Kaiser, and all the rest of them. They have a new gas on this sector, the result of which is to produce broncho-pneumonia combined wih boils and blisters. Pleasant, isn't it? Especially as the stuff usually lies about for a bit before anyone knows it's there. At times it is necessary to keep respirators on for hours. But I believe our experts have got the stuff ticketed now, and no doubt protective measures will soon be forthcoming.

[Lombartzyde]
19 August, 1917

We came up to reserve line on Thursday [15 August], and are to be 6 days here and 6 days in the front line. I was sent up in advance to take over for D company, and came up in the afternoon with two N.C.O.'s. We got a motor carry about halfway, and had to walk the rest with shell-fire going on; two bursts came quite close and we got the wind up a bit, but fortunately we found a covered communication trench alongside the road which went nearly all the way and gave us at least cover from view.

The reserve trenches here are A1, with very fine dug-outs; but it is a hot part, and I've begun to realize there is a war on. The German 'five-nines' keep potting in incessantly, sometimes every few seconds, and make a hades of a row. We are close beside a town which they have been shelling for the last month or so; I wish you could see it.

On Friday I had to go round and visit the other battalion headquarters, to see where they were. It was no joke, as we were exposed every now and then, and plenty of stuff was coming over. At one of the headquarters locations I saw a dug-out where 16 men of the battalion we relieved were all killed with one shell last week. Their grave was made simply by closing up the entrance and wiring it round. On Friday night I was detailed to take a carrying party of 50 men to the H.E. dump [high explosive shells] over in the town. All one gets is a map reference; then we have to find the place in the dark, the route being chiefly along trenches and tunnels – every place is so smashed up that you can't tell when you've arrived unless someone is there. We had a good deal of excitement, as just when we started off some 'whiz-bangs' began coming over and landing about 100 yards away. We had to 'beat it' for cover until things quietened down. When we got into the town the Bosche had just got well under way with gas shells and H.E. mixed. We put on our respirators and popped into the tunnels again; it was nearly an hour before we could come out. We made four trips across the river with stuff for the support line, using a bridge which was a crazy collection of boarding strung together, about as strong as orange boxes; on one of our journeys a shell landed in the water perhaps 50 yards away. We have had four casualties since we came up, but nothing serious. It is certainly remarkable how few men get hit, as the bits of jagged cast-iron that come flying about sometimes could go right through you.

Last night I was on a working party improving one of the communication trenches. I saw a bit where the revetting material was being forced forward by a pile of earth and told a man to get up and dig it out. He jumped up, stuck in his spade, and then said in a husky voice, 'It's a body, sir'. That sort of thing fairly puts the wind up one, on a pitch dark night, when all the illumination is the frequent flash from guns or signal lights, and courage at these times gets a bit shaky. However, it's wonderful how you get used to it. We do very little all day but eat and sleep, all the work being done at night. The weather is very fine and dry, and I sincerely hope that continues for the time we are in the front line as there is very little shelter up there; the whole place is badly knocked about. Both sides keep an eye on any improvements made in the front line and promptly unimprove it, as much as they can.

[Lombartzyde]
22 August, 1917

We are going into the front line tonight. Last night Caldwell[19] and I had to go up and have a look round, as our platoons are taking the front of our company. Just before we were due to start old Fritz began straffing just beside us with high explosive shell (5.9 and 8″). His planes must have seen something, for he just about got the range and for an hour or so we had an awful time. It's no joke. That picture of Bairnsfather's, 'Where did that one go', was acted in character several times ... [CENSORED] ... These were got out at once, but at great danger, and I saw one of them go past on a stretcher; what with mud and blood he wasn't nice to look at. I heard he had all his ribs broken. Poor beggar, he looked as if he was going farther than Blighty.

After things cooled off a bit we got started on our trip up, about 1000 yards. There are only fragments of trench left here and there, and when we got up to about 400 yards the Bosche lights got a bit dangerous, as we were in the open and every time one went up (about every minute or so) we had to flop down. A bit further on we got a machine gun on us (probably unaimed), and we lay flat and listened to the whistle of the bullets passing over us, the first actual experience of the kind I've had. So the journey was a series of short rushes in between the flares and bursts of M.G. fire, but we arrived O.K. finally. The line up there is not trenches at all, on account of the watery ground, but breastworks. These have mostly been blown to atoms, so that nothing much remains but a series of concrete emplacements in which we crouch during the day, and from which we emerge at night to do repair work, and patrols. But anything in the way of repairs is sure to be knocked out next morning.

I've got about the worst position in the battalion, as 13 platoon is on the extreme left and the Bosche is holding the same line on our left, the space between us being only about 40 yards. We used to hold the 'trench' but half of it was lost about two months ago. I hope he hasn't any designs on the other half. As a matter of fact the ground in between is a honeycomb of shell-holes all full of water, so it would be pretty difficult for either of us to surprise the other. But in my opinion he's a jolly sight too near. As well as having him on our left, we have of course his main line in front at a distance of 40 to 80 yards; but the officer I'm taking over from told me that his [the German] position, etc., was a sight worse than ours, and I expect the Hun is a lot more unhappy and afraid of us than we are of him. When I was up the officer was just going on patrol. He was armed with his revolver and two Mills bombs, and the N.C.O. had a most villainous-looking 'knobkerry'. The job is usually to creep over and find what the Hun is doing without being seen, although sometimes they have 'fighting patrols' when they want a prisoner for information. One of the disadvantages of patrols is that the other side is quite likely to have one out too, and as you can believe, it is rather an eerie job, considering that the ground in front has a few corpses here and there. I believe there is a Bosche one on the wire in front of my centre post, and several attempts have been made to bring it in to our lines for identification of unit, etc; but the corpse's pals have it covered with an M.G., and so far it hasn't been pinched. Perhaps we'll have a try, although that doesn't appeal to me personally. Meanwhile of course every day it's getting 'higher', especially in the hot weather.

Last night there were two wounded waiting to be carried down (you can imagine what the stretcher-bearers' job is like up there), but I believe there isn't a great deal doing. A few trench mortar 'mediums' came over last night and shook us up a bit but did no more. On our way back they started gas shelling a bridge we had to get back over. I can tell you I was mighty happy when we got safely into the fold again. But of course we do it all over again tonight, plus the platoon; and if Hans gets an idea there's a relief in progress he will let us know about it.

I just heard yesterday about Bobbie.[20] I wrote Auntie, but there is nothing to say. What awful bad luck she has had. I don't know how she will stand this blow. I must try to go up to Stornoway for a day when I get leave, and I hinted that I might do so.

[Lombartzyde]
25 August, 1917

This has been an eventful day for me as I have had my first real scrap. I had more excitement in an hour this morning than I've had all the rest of my life put together. Just before dawn the sentry at my end post gave a yell, 'Stand to, they're coming over'. As a matter of fact it wasn't an attack in force but only a small patrol with one officer which he had spotted. I grabbed my revolver and rushed up to find my Lewis gun going like blazes and shots coming flying in at us from the enemy at about ten yards range. Their officer dashed round the corner of the trench at point blank range, and he dropped at our feet badly wounded. Some of my lot got started with bombs and I got in three shots myself, the joint result being that the Bosche hit the trail for home less one man, who at present is lying dead just beyond our post. We will get him in tonight and give him the order of the wooden cross. I had time now to turn my attention to the officer, who was dripping blood; when he saw me approach with my revolver he got the wind up properly, and shrieked out 'Kamerad, Kamerad, don't shoot, I'm German officer!' which shows what he expected. I got the stretcher bearers to fix his wound up a bit and asked him a few questions. He was only 20, and had the Iron Cross; he was in the 3rd Regiment of Marine Infantry. He was moaning and groaning all the time, so I got him sent down the line to H.Q., first deducting as souvenirs his cap (just like the Crown Prince's), his Iron Cross ribbon, and his gas mask. This is the biggest piece of luck I've had for many a long day, as D company had been detailed to go over the top tonight to bring back prisoners so that the unit opposite could be identified, and now we have an A1 prisoner without leaving our own fireside. A couple of hours later my sergeant hopped over and took the pack, etc., of the corpse in front, and the contents provided beaucoup souvenirs for the men, and one or two for me, as well as ample identification of the unit in the shape of addresses on letters, etc.

Yesterday afternoon I had another slight adventure. We suspected that the nearest Bosche trench (about 50 yards in front) was evacuated during the day as we had noticed men coming in at dusk and leaving at dawn. My sergeant and I crawled carefully across No Man's Land and had a look in and found no one but a dead Hun. I think we must have been seen, however, as last night when they arrived they started bombing up their own trench, so they must have suspected that someone was there. I am hoping we'll be relieved from the front line tonight and go back to support, although up here during the day it is very quiet as a rule. At night we get M.G. fire, rifle grenades, trench mortars, minnenwerfer [heavy mortar shells], and life becomes a series of explosions. The ground up here is something terrible, all shell holes full of water almost touching one another, and many dead in front in various stages of corruption so that the atmosphere is foul. I have been out patrolling in front twice; it is a rotten job, as you can imagine, under these circumstances. Well, I'll stop now as I must have a sleep before evening . . . .

[Capelle, S of Dunkerque]
30 August, 1917

We were relieved on Monday night and came down to a small village where we stayed the night, and then the following day came on here by motor lorries. We are however leaving here again tomorrow, and I understand we are going further back; but no one has any idea of what we are to do. Your two packets of papers were waiting for me on Monday night and I am much obliged for them. My last two nights in the line and the night we left were all very unpleasant, as you can judge from the following details.

Saturday. We got a message that relief would be carried out at 10.30 by another company. About nine the Bosche attacked the company on our right, which at once sent up S.O.S. for artillery support. [21] Our artillery started a terrific bombardment along the whole front, but on our section they unfortunately had the range short a little, with the result that we got it – and of course in a few minutes the German guns were going like blazes too. For two hours we had a rain of shells on us at over 100 or so a minute, and we crouched in our concrete dugouts wondering when a direct hit would happen and blow us all to bits. Three of my men were hit and we had to take down sentries and everything, although the Bosche was just over the way, so you can imagine how happy we were. Of course the relief was impossible, and it was 2.30 a.m. before we got started on our way down to support. When we did my guide lost his way, and we all had to lie down in the open until he found where he was. Support line is very uncomfortable, with small and muddy dugouts – but we were thankful to get in.

Sunday. About 7.30 p.m. a heavy minnenwefer shell landed seven yards from the entrance to our dugout with a noise like a gasometer [petrol storage tank] going up, and for a minute there was a terrific shower of stones, earth, and all sorts of debris. Fritz has a habit of repeating himself, so we got out and scooted along the trench about 100 yards, not wishing to be buried alive. In a minute or so someone shouted, 'Here's another coming!' I looked up and saw the comet-like tail which these things leave coming apparently straight for us. I flattened myself up against the trench (no use getting under cover) and thought of dear old Broadway, and in a moment heard the brute hit the ground and go off, and was again covered with flying earth, etc., but fortunately nothing worse. However, there was a shout for stretcher bearers and shovels, and I found that some poor wretch had been blown right into the air and had landed right in the centre of the crater, which consisted of soft slimy mud, about 15 feet across, and was up to his armpits in it. The rain was pouring down and water was running into the crater like anything. Before we could get started on relief measures he had only his head showing above water and his yells were awful – we discovered later that his leg was broken and he had two wounds. It was very difficult to get to him at all and we had to make a sort of gangway of trench boards for the men who were holding his head up and for the shovellers, and one for a line of men passing buckets to bail out the water. After three hours' work we had made no progress whatever, as the mud kept slipping in, and you can imagine what a dickens of a job it was as shells were coming over all the while, and any minute might have scattered the lot of us. I phoned for a medical orderly and some choloroform as I thought we would have to let him go. But in the meantime Capt. McLellan had sent for some of the R.E. [Royal Engineers], who now arrived with a pump and ropes and got started on a scientific basis. Ultimately, in about another three hours, the man was pulled out, looking like nothing on earth. I don't think he will live. We were all soaked to the skin and I was in mud over the knees (and trench mud is *mud*), but of course we had no other clothes, no fires, and only the dugout to sit in. I went to sleep sitting up; next morning it was fine and windy, and I got pretty well dried up.

Monday. Relieved by platoons. I got instructions to proceed to [illegible] about 18 kilos away and await the rest of the company; arrived there about 4.30 a.m. and found that after I left, orders were cancelled and I should have gone to a place six miles back. The men were dead to the world and couldn't possibly have gone another mile, so I had to start looking for a billet and get food. Next morning we joined up with the battalion. How's all that for three pleasant evenings?

On getting in here yesterday I got a billet with a bed in it, and I slept from 9 p.m. to 8 a.m. today, the first time I've had my clothes off for two weeks. By the way, our little 'do' the other morning appeared in the Corps and Divisional 'Summary of Information', with some information they got from the wounded officer at H.Q. Capt. Sussex was killed in the attack on B company on Saturday, but he is the only officer casualty this time . . . .

Stornoway
20 September, 1917

I have been doing some travelling since I last wrote you. My leave came through nine days ago, along with Nicol's, and we both cleared off instantaneously and got to Boulogne last Wednesday. We left there at 7:30 a.m. on Thursday, reached Folkestone at 9:15, London 12:30, and Glasgow at 11:45 p.m. I got my warrant for Stornoway and got the two extra days allowed for the Hebrides, so I'm not due to arrive in France until Tuesday. I left Glasgow by the 4:35 a.m. train on Tuesday and arrived here at 11 that night. The crossing was very bad and I had the usual rotten time, and am, in fact, just recovering now – in time for my return journey tonight.

Yesterday I took Auntie [i.e., Mrs Mackenzie] for a drive to Callanish in the afternoon per motor. It was pretty cold but I think she enjoyed it all right. We had tea in a house there before coming back and the woman was saying that 18 have gone from that village. I thought she meant that 18 had joined up and I thought that was very good, but it appeared she meant 18 killed, including her own son.

The boat leaves about 3 in the morning and I'll be in Glasgow late on Friday night. I shall go up to London on Saturday and have Sunday and Monday there. I'm going out to Mr Jeffrey's [22] house for dinner on Sunday but otherwise have the time to myself. The leave train is at 7:50 a.m. on Tuesday from Victoria, and I'll be in France that afternoon, but it will take about a couple of days to find the battalion as they are in the line just now.

Grosvenor Hotel, London
24 September, 1917

I am spending two days here on my way back. Yesterday I spent the afternoon and evening with Mr. Jeffrey. He lives at Palmer's Green, which is over an hour's run on the bus from here and I saw a bit more of London that way. Today I have been strolling round buying a few things I required. I am going up to Frascati's for lunch, and then to the matinée at the Palladium. In the evening I am going to see H.B. Irving's new play and tomorrow morning I get the 7:30 special for Folkestone.

I see the Ypres offensive came off all right and I just missed the worst of that, I think. The battalion was marching up to that neighbourhood two days after I left and I hope they have done their little bit before I get back. I don't expect I'll find them until about Thursday or Friday.

Today I saw a U.S. naval officer in the Strand, the first official American I've seen; but I suppose there are plenty of them here now. Weather is lovely; I always seem to strike it lucky that way in London. The hotel is near Buckingham Palace and yesterday morning the guard passed with the full band. I think there is nothing to touch that as a military spectacle. But London is full of fine sights – military and otherwise.

> *[Maclean returned to the 1st Battalion on 28 September. While he was on leave, the battalion had played an important role in the fierce and confused fighting for the Ypres-Menin Road and Polygon Wood, particularly south of Zonnebeke from 24 to 27 September. Initially assigned to Divisional Reserve, while the Anzac Corps assaulted Polygon Wood, the 19th Brigade was drawn into the battle on 26 September, when B company of the 1st Battalion attacked with the 100th Brigade early that morning. Later in the day two companies regained ground north of the Menin Road and, with the 100th Brigade repelled a series of determined German counter-attacks. In these operations four officers and 119 men of the 1st Battalion were killed or wounded. Subsequently the battalion held positions in the newly-captured line east of Messines, and, from 6 November until early December, in the Passchendaele salient (for the divisional historian, an experience of particular 'unpleasantness and horror'). The letters of this period are marked by self-questioning and gloom, relieved only by deepening admiration for the character and resilience of the British soldier.]*

['Bristol Castle' area
between Messines and Warneton]
13 October, 1917

Since last writing you I have been having a dickens of a time. On arrival at our rest area last Friday after a 16 or 17 mile march, we got the pleasing news that plans were changed and we would proceed next morning to entraining point and return to a place ['Bedford Camp'] a mile or two behind the line. The journey took a whole day up to midnight. On Monday morning we came up to Brigade Reserve and that evening moved up to the front line. It was raining and blowing, and very cold, and the march up to the trenches was the frigid limit. We had to go along miles (literally) of communication trenches in the dark, and as every now and then we struck a shell hole or a bit that had been blown in and had to be climbed over, and as everywhere except the 'duckboards' was deep in slime and mud, you can imagine what we were like. The last 300 yards or so had to be done over the open across clayey ground; it was a regular acrobatic performance getting along as it was very slippery and 'holey'. I fell right into half-filled shell-holes three or four times, and soon exhausted all the swear words I ever heard, and was reduced to vulgar blasphemy. We took five hours to get up and arrived soaking wet, covered with filthy mud and perfectly miserable. My platoon had a series of isolated posts to hold, so I took these over and mounted the various garrisons. My own residence was a hole cut out of the side of the trench, just big enough to take me in the prone position, with a water-proof sheet hanging in front to keep out the weather – in which duty it failed miserably. The trench itself, in which my posts were, had an average of 9 inches to a foot of mud and water, owing to the rain; we were all provided with rubber thigh boots which kept our feet fairly dry, but which accumulated pounds of mud, and my 'cubby hole' received most of that. So it wasn't exactly a comfortable place.

The very first night Fritz came over and raided one of my posts. He got round the back of it somehow and took it in the rear, chucked in a bomb, jumped in (six of them) grabbed two men, shot another, and bolted back again. I was at another post at the time and you can imagine how cheered I was when I came round and heard the glad tidings. It certainly made us a bit jumpy for the rest of the time. The Bosche line was from 50 to 150 yards distant and we could hear them singing and moving about in some places. We had two machine guns and a sniper opposite us; but he did no damage with them, and we had a pot at him occasionally. During the four days I was quite on my own except for a nocturnal visit from the company commander, and I certainly felt very anxious and worried all the time. We 'stood to' all night and slept during the day (sentries with periscopes, of course), and filled in spare time improving the defences. I got my rations nightly, usually in a filthy wet sandbag and generally consisting of one excessively filthy loaf, a tin of sausages or bully, COLD (business of shuddering), some jam or cheese, and a candle. My only implement was my pocket clasp knife. For drink we had the rum issue, and we got water once; and I also had a flask of whisky. It rained every blessed day. I discovered the acme of human misery – stand to at 4.15 a.m., wet, muddy, dark, cold, hungry, thirsty, and with half a chance of a scrap with the Hun for breakfast. Of course, that gentle person no doubt was experiencing much the same sensations.

Last night when we were relieved it was just such another night as when we went in, and the journey down was a swearing competition. The relief was four hours late in arriving, and we finally got back to the reserve trenches about dawn this morning. Here we have A1 dug-outs. Caldwell and I share one measuring at least 6' × 6' × 4', which seems like a palace now. We shall be here about [CENSORED] days, and hope to get back to rest camp for about [CENSORED] days; and after that I suppose will be up here again. I got my first wash and shave for [CENSORED] days this morning, and also a pukka hot breakfast of tea and bacon; and feel that I wouldn't change places with J.P. Morgan – such is the power of comparison.

You would have been amused to have seen our four company officers when we arrived this morning. The usual caricature of a tramp just about shows it – bearded, matted hair, torn and filthy clothes, boots and puttees indistinguishable, etc. But now we are like Christians again. I got mail here, including your letter of 23 September, and a copy of *The Radiator*[23], both of which I was very glad to have. I note you are persistently optimistic as to an early finish of the war, but I'm afraid it will take a bit longer than you appear to think, although I have no doubt we shall down the Hun all right. He has been getting an awful straffing round Ypres way lately . . . (CENSORED) . . . The bombardment up there is something incredible; at night the flash of the guns makes a continuous light in the sky, while the sound approaches that of the roll of a kettledrum. It must be simply damnable for him. Half a dozen moderate-sized shells in quick succession will, as I well know, put the wind up any old troops. To get hours of it must drive him off his chump.

I long for the piping times of peace again, and I shall be very happy when, if ever, they come again. No one but a lunatic enjoys a life like this. When I get the chance I intend to make up, and a bit, for the present discomforts. However, it doesn't do to moan and groan meantime. And it might be worse.

[Neuve Eglise]
26 October, 1917

... We came back from our labour job [repairing roads and railways] two days ago and I wasn't sorry, as with the weather we had, living in tents wasn't an ideal existence, to say nothing of the daily and nightly [aerial] bombing. We had one man killed and several wounded by a bomb ... The last working party I was on up there was right in the middle of a group of howitzers; I had a good chance of watching them firing, and that was interesting although the noise and concussion is awful. On the way up that morning two dead soldiers were carried past us; one had died en route and was lying on his face on the stretcher in a pool of blood, with his back bare, and a big wound in his back half-filled with a field dressing. It was a horrible sight. I wish the people responsible for the way could see a few things like that . . . .

[Neuve Eglise]
28 October, 1917

Yours of September 28th reached me this afternoon. I note you were returning from holidays. I hope you had better weather for the run home than you were expecting and that you got comfortably settled. After this war it will take me about five minutes to settle down in any old place, from the time I arrive. I also received a copy of *The American*[24], which is O.K. You are surprised that I prefer the (comparatively) 'heavy stuff', but what we require frequently is something to pass the time; a paper like *Life*, etc., lasts me about ten minutes. I shall be very glad to have the book you mention, and I'm obliged to you for sending it.

I am having my last two days of rest prior to another tour in the line. Today (Sunday), which, by the way, you may remember is the third anniversary of the day I left New York, is the first fine day here for a long time. I had the afternoon free and went with two or three other officers into [CENSORED (pehaps Armentières)] a fair-sized French town about seven miles back. On these journeys we just take our chance of a lift on a motor lorry as there are always plenty going back and forward from the front. There were some pretty decent shops, an 'E.F.C.' (Expeditionary Force Canteen), and an officers' club, so we did some shopping and had tea and then hiked back along the road until the first lorry came along . . . .

One of our officers – and a second loot at that – has got the

D.S.O. this week.[25] It was for a stunt at Ypres when he and his platoon were lent to another battalion during a push. They had advanced a bit but were held up by a Bosche 'pill box' with about 30 or 40 Germans in it, and bristling with M.G.'s. While some of the other officers were making up their minds, Preston took his platoon and rushed the place. He lost ten men on the way over, but when he arrived the Huns 'kameraded' – but not before about half of them, including two officers, were killed. The job was worth a Victoria Cross. But in this war the man who gets the V.C. has got to be a D fool, and have the devil's own luck as well. However, it was certainly a great credit to our battalion. Last night Preston was around here with another B company officer, playing Miller and I at bridge. He had his ribbon up, and gave us a full account of the affair; I can tell you he had some excitement. The Bosche trench at the place where the strong point was, was full of dead British soldiers; Preston's crowd had to walk over them when they rushed the pill-box. When I hear of exploits like that I sometimes think I must be a deuce of a coward. But one never knows what one could do on the spur of the moment. Perhaps I wouldn't absolutely 'beat it'.

[Hamburg, E of Ypres]
28 November, 1917

I was very glad to get your letter of 5 November today, the first letter I've had for a bit. We've been up there again, and well beyond the limits of civilization this time. I'll try to give you some account of the past week or ten days. It may give you some idea of what the British Tommy is trying to do. Only I hope you won't think I'm trying to elicit sympathy for myself, or grousing in any way. But life in the line on a 'push front' is simply hell; no one denies that.

We did a few days of rest about ten days ago, and then came up in motor buses to our position as brigade support. In due course the turn of our brigade came; we went up first for a day, as battalion in support, then did three in the front line, and are now back as support battalion again. While in support we are in dugouts on the face of a hill, the whole surface of which has been and is still being pounded to blazes by Fritz's heavies, at intervals. The first day there we had two killed and two wounded, and today one more wounded; and that is a long way from the front line. Last night a couple of shells landed outside . . . [(unidentified)] skedaddled and I was left in entire possession (our other two officers were casualties two days ago – one shell-shocked, one accidentally wounded). The dug-out consists of a hole in the mud; but it is roofed over with beams and is splinter-proof. I have two duck-boards for a floor, and my servant has 'won' a bundle of sandbags which form a bed, for such times as I have a chance to use it. I'm pretty comfortable except for the ever-present fear that a 5.9 is going to land on it. But I've just one day more, and I have strong hopes. The surrounding ground, over which much fighting has taken place, is one mass of mud, water, and shell-holes – not a tree or a house (except Bosche pill-boxes) left standing for miles. It all looks most desolate, expecially at dusk. Ten yards behind my dug-out a shell has dug up an old Bosche corpse. It has the right leg lying across the left shoulder, and is not beautiful. But we get used to these sights.

The trip to the front line from here is (naturally) dangerous, but we were fortunate and got up, without a casualty, to our company H.Q. in the village – some village: absolutely flat and with dead men every ten or a dozen yards. I can tell you one has the 'wind up' properly making a journey along there on a relief night: hurry along is the order of the day. We had Capt. McLellan, Caldwell, Goble, and myself, and I got the job of taking the front line posts for the first 24 hours – no proper trench, and no movement possible during the day, no shelter from the rain, cold food only. The next night I got down to company H.Q. to find Goble had gone down injured; and just as I got in a message arrived, 'All B company officers knocked out, send Caldwell to take over'. That left only me, so I had to go straight back to the front line and carry on. I can tell you I was 'the fed-up stuff'. The same night a sergeant and one man in the next post to the one I was in at the time were killed by a shell, and others were landing all round us while we crouched in the bottom of our 'ole' and wished the little hate would hurry up and stop. I don't mind saying that on such occasions one is afraid – the bravest man on earth would be. But after all, the chances are well in our favour, as it would take a direct hit in the trench to knock you out in most cases, except for unlucky splinters. We were relieved last night, and didn't half put our skates on coming down here (through the usual mud and with the usual cursing); but this moring at 7 I had to go up again as far as battalion H.Q. with a big ration party. After that I had rifle inspection, and rum issue; and have had the afternoon free to watch the shells bursting. By the way, the amount of rum and whisky I've drunk in the past three days would shock you. But it's necessary. We get a jar of rum per company every day, and occasionally get a little extra 'on the side'. When one comes down through a shelled area, a good stiff drink is the first thing one wants. You find very few teetotallers out here.

Today the rain has stopped, and I have been getting my coat and other clothes dried up a bit. Last night we all just lay down and slept as we were, wet and muddy. I haven't shaved or washed for a week now; I look like a Bosche prisoner. But I hope soon to alter that. One great trouble just now is the cold. The men have all been issued their leather jerkins; I got one of these for this trip and found it splendid, but of course I had my coat as well, which the men hadn't. A dry pair of socks makes a huge difference in comfort; trench boots are good also as they keep out water pretty well, and are better than puttees for mud. But the cold, and conditions generally, were so bad that we relieved the men in the posts every 24 hours. By the time they were about due to go out, they were quite ready for it, especially in the new posts we made (the old ones were the acme of discomfort).

I must say I have acquired a huge amount of affection and regard for the British soldier. Some of them grouse a lot, but that is often excusable. The average type is a good cheery chap who can stick a deuce of a lot, and who is generally very grateful if he sees you are doing your best for him.

Well, I think we're booked for a rest very soon now. We're all hoping for a good one, as we've done a good bit of shell-dodging in the past six weeks or so, and in our own opinions think we've earned a week or two in some bon town with 'swell cafes' and such things. Perhaps we may get that before doing another tour: I hope so, and we may be lucky enough to have it during the festive season. Don't waste too much sympathy on me, then, as we stand a good chance of being 'out'. I might even land my second spell of leave about then – but not likely since I'm well up on the list, owing to casualties; this last trip we had five officer casualties, which makes a difference in my position on the leave list. Perhaps I'll spend *next* Christmas with you. But as the pessimist says, 'I recollect your saying so about this time last year'. However we'll hope for it anyhow. At times I feel very depressed over the whole business; but we have our good times too now and then, and if I come through it all safely, it will be a great experience to look back on. However, as one man said today in my hearing, 'If I have a dog after the war and I see it following the soldiers, I'll shoot it'. Them's my sentiments.

Yes, I got Mr. Moir's[26] letter a long time ago and replied to it. Let me know if he didn't get my letter, please, and I shall write again.

I guess that American who was lecturing you had the right idea. I've felt that 'over the top' sensation (in the pit of the tummy is the place) – but not the actual going over, as our little show was cancelled. But believe me, going over the top is only one of the things that go to make up the excitement of life here . . . .

[Brandhoek]
4 December, 1917

. . . The men have a fearful lot of stuff to carry, especially when going up to the line, as they usually then have a day's rations and also such things as bags of bombs and Lewis gun magazines to carry, in addition to their usual load. But the man I'm sorry for is the No. 1 on the Lewis who carries the blasted thing itself. I can tell you I've often wondered how the dickens he ever gets it up. Fortunately my No. 1 is a giant, about 6 ft. 4, a bricklayer by trade who thinks nothing of it. But his language when he 'steps on a stair that isn't there' and gets a mud bath is pretty much to the point. He is one of my best men and a right good sort . . . .

[Watou, 6 mi. W of Poperinghe]
12 December, 1917

Yesterday we came back by train and road to rest billets, and can now look forward to a few weeks of civilisation and comfort; very welcome, as we have not really been out of the forward area for nearly three months. Our billets are very scattered and not near any big town, so we aren't too pleased. I was very unfortunate in being allotted one which turned out to belong to another battalion; I had to clear out of it at 8 p.m. last night, and spent the night in my valise on the stone floor of our company mess. I was particularly annoyed as I had to give way to a padre, who has probably been living in ease and comfort while we were in the line; he was certainly very aggressive about it. When I told him I intended to remain where I was until I got an order to quit from my own C.O., he said he would see I was turned out whether I was in bed or not – and otherwise exhibited a meek and Christian demeanour. I shall make a point of sleeping ostentatiously at his next service. Most chaplains out here are nothing but a nuisance, occupying good billets and drinking our drinks, and doing nothing noticeable for the spiritual welfare of the troops. As a class they are cordially disliked, with few exceptions.

Our company mess is in a farm of the usual French, or Belgian, type, consisting of a huge dung-heap surrounded by buildings, all more or less filthy. Cows and pigs walk about unrestrained, and mud is plentiful. This room we have, however, is quite clean, and with a good wood fire we are very comfortable, especially as we have a very good cook just now. We expect to have a great dinner on Christmas Eve. One officer has two pheasants coming, and the others all expect parcels with the other necessary items. The officer first mentioned, by the way, is our company knut, a London society man who knows Lady Diana Manners and other eminent people of that description. He is quite an amusing person.[27]

Weather here is very cold now but it doesn't affect us so much now that we are under a roof again. The last day we were up I was on a working party, making a plank road for the artillery, and old Fritz started dropping souvenirs as well as firing on us with M.G.'s from his aeroplanes. It is rather a disagreeable sensation, when one is going out the next day. But no harm was done. There is a lot of aeroplane activity round about this section. When we were in the front line the Bosche planes used to come over sometimes looking for our posts, and flying so low that we could make out the pilots quite easily. I have seen several of them brought down, and that's a fine sight – except, perhaps, when the old Hun himself tumbles out, which isn't too nice to see. They go in a lot for bombing our back areas but don't do a great deal of damage. One camp we were in was bombed after the night we left it, and all the horses of a battalion – about 50 – were killed or badly hurt. But I don't think there will be anything of that here, as we are not even in a village.

[From 20 December until early in the New Year Maclean and Nicol were assigned to train company 'specialists' in bombing and the Lewis gun; meanwhile, the battalion manned trenches on the Menin Road and the Passchendaele ridge, and provided working parties.]

[Watou]
23 December, 1917

At present I am having an A1 time. There are just Nicol, myself and the Transport Officer left here. Nicol and I mess together in D company's farm, and as we both believe in living while the living's good we do ourselves well. We have a cook and two servants and get jolly good meals. We have about 80 men here altogether, and we are giving them a Christmas dinner of the usual fare, together with a barrel of beer and some fags. We bought eight four-pound plum puddings at the Expeditionary Force canteen yesterday, and we are also going to give each man an egg for breakfast on Christmas morning. So there will be considerable peace and goodwill on the day.

Today, Sunday, we rose at nine, by which time my servant (an ex-London fireman) had a fine fire on and breakfast ready. I'm getting D company's 'charger' at eleven, and Nicol and I will go for a ride until lunch time. The weather is cold; hard frost, but just the thing for this season of the year. On working days our hours are 9–12 only. I do one hour lecture, one hour physical drill and bayonet-fighting, and one hour 'pooping off' bombs. We fired about 30 yesterday morning, and it is quite good fun. So far absolutely no one has been here to see that we are doing any work at all, but we may get a visitor from Brigade H.Q. any time, so we have to keep up to scratch. On Christmas Day we will join up for dinner with the Transport Officer and the interpreter, both of whom are living on their own at present, and I expect there will be considerable liquor consumed, as the T.O. is not a teetotaller. I was over at his billet last night and he had 12 bottles of gin (a new case) ranged along the wall. However, as long as he gives us horses to ride I don't mind his habits. He was 'mentioned' [in despatches] in the latest list from H.Q. but I don't know why.

I expect this little holiday will last about a week; after the battalion returns we shall have a few more days, then hit the trail for the unpleasant places again. We can hear the guns here but are well away from them, and as this isn't even a village we don't get bombed either; so it's a real rest for us, and we can do with it.

You asked about 'pill-boxes'. These were originally nicknamed 'pillar-boxes', but that has got corrupted into 'pill-boxes', which is what they are always called now. They are very strong, made of reinforced concrete; there is nothing in front but the slits for machine guns. The entrance is behind, so that any ones we get (and we have hundreds of them) have to be converted, as the Bosche has the map reference of every one, and has been known more than once to land a shell right into the door, with disturbing results. You were also asking if I ever come across Parker.[28] He is in the 5th Scottish Rifles and I have met him several times since he came out. He is pretty senior, being an old Territorial, and just now is doing second-in-command while the other man is on leave. We are getting a new C.O. shortly ourselves; the present C.O., Major

Scott, will be second-in-command. It is very remarkable how many changes take place among the officers of a battalion out here. Nicol and I were counting up the other day and found that 20 officers have left the battalion since we came. So we have lasted quite a while, comparatively.

[Maclean went on leave, to Glasgow and London, from 5 to 22 January, 1918.]

[Brandhoek]
26 January, 1918

I left London on Monday, spent Tuesday night in Calais, and arrived back with the battalion on Wednesday evening. I got a bit of a dull thud as I found that on account of the recent bad weather the programme existing when I left had been modified, and that the battalion was going up to the front line for a final spasm before the Division came out.[29] We left the following night and were in for two days only, coming out last night; but that is quite enough under the conditions existing up there. I was in charge of two posts which were just 'improved' shell holes, with no shelter or overhead cover, and of course muddy. The weather was good, except for the first night, when it rained for about two hours, and it was also very cold. As the general position of our line of posts is not known to the enemy, we have to be quiet all day (especially when his planes are overhead), and this gets very monotonous; one longs for darkness, when one can stand up and stretch – even though that is the dangerous time. We were quite close to the Fritzes, and at night could see their working parties quite plainly, working on their wire. Yesterday morning early, two of them of an inquisitive turn of mind came strolling over in our direction; we were all lying doggo, waiting to gather them in, when they changed direction and went over towards the post on the left. The silly fools got up to welcome them, and it turned out that they had no intention of coming in; they immediately turned and ran like blazes for home, which they reached quite safely, although of course they were fired on. I could have got them quite easily if I had only known what was going to happen, as all we had to do was to pop out and sneak up behind them.

We had a fairly quiet trip this time as regards shelling, but were bothered a lot by machine-gun fire. Last night there was a brilliant

moon, and I thought our relief would be spotted, especially as
earlier in the evening the Bosche had been running his M.G.'s
along our front a good deal, so that we thought he had seen
something. But we got away quietly. We had about two hours' walk
down the duck-boards and then went back about ten miles on the
light railway (open trucks) to one of the camps. We got in about 1
a.m. and after having some grub, and issuing rum, I got to bed and
slept until 10 a.m. this morning. I was very tired, as during the last
48 hours I have not been asleep at all. We expect to go back for a
rest now, and should have a fairly decent time for a few weeks.

Just now our pipe band is playing up and down outside the huts.
It is one of the best in France. Last night we had the company
pipers with us coming down, but it's a bit ludicrous, as the men are
all so done up there's no such thing as keeping step or anything of
that sort – although the pipes certainly buck one up considerably.
Coming down, of course, everyone although pretty well tired out is
feeling happy with the prospect of good hot meals and rest. This
trip my servant forgot to bring up my muffler and wool helmet,
which didn't help matters; but he is generally an A1 chap, very
cheerful, who will do any amount of work for me.

I had a very good time while I was in London. I 'clicked' for duty
again on the boat going over, but my job only arose in the event of
being torpedoed; so I had nothing to do. At Calais I spent the night
at the Hotel Sauvage, supposed to be the best; but pretty rotten if it
is. These French hotels, except in really big towns, are punk. The
only decent meal is dinner . . . .

[St. Martin au Laert, a suburb of St. Omer]
31 January, 1918

We have come back by train to a billeting area, and at the
moment of writing I am very well off, with about the best billet I've
had since I came to France. It is in an 'estaminet', and I have a
good-sized room with a good bed; and the people are very nice. We
are near a good town so there is some amusement to be had, and as
we expect to be here for a few weeks things look quite rosy. I see a
good many Americans about here, but not the main body of
troops, which is elsewhere.

D company got a bit of an acquisition since coming here in the
person of a new officer – Cole – who was one of the first violinists
in the Scottish Orchestra.[30] He knows all the musical 'knuts' and is
a most interesting chap. He was conductor of the Glasgow
amateur orchestra; I expect you may have heard of him. We have

now a full complement of officers in the company, which makes things easier. White (the Signals Officer) told me that I am probably to be sent to the Corps Signalling School for the next course, starting about the beginning of March. It is a six weeks' course, and absolutely 'the goods'. I sincerely hope it comes off. As White expects to get a transfer to the [Divisional] Signals Company, I should probably succeed him here. My signalling knowledge is much out of date now, as many changes and improvements have been introduced since I did any of that kind of work; a signalling officer has to be a sort of electrical engineer. But a six weeks' course would put me all right.

Weather here is very fine just now although it is sharp and frosty. We have training parades from 9 to 3, and are finished after that. They started a riding school (7-8a.m.), but the first morning the Transport Officer told me I needn't attend. We had some excitement that morning as the horses were all very fresh, and almost everyone was thrown. In fact four of the horses galloped back to the stables without their riders, causing a bit of commotion in the village street. I can't ride very well yet, but at the school all they aim at is to enable you to ride with a decent seat in a moderate way; we don't get any jumping or anything like that. Our T.O. is a Canadian and a very hard case. He is very unpopular; but he seems to like me all right, which probably accounts for my being passed out . . . .

[St. Martin au Laert]
10 February, 1918

I was glad to receive your long letter of 21 January, and I have also received some papers, including an insurance one with extracts from my letters. Thompson[31] sent me a copy of *The Mutual Life Quarterly* containing the same thing.

I'm enjoying the rest out here very much. The weather has been ideal most of the time, and were it not for fairly steady work it would be almost as good as being on leave. The town nearby is a typical old French town of the picturesque type, with quaint streets and old churches; one might forget all about the war except for the numerous soldiers – not to mention the German prisoners' camp. The latter do a lot of work round here and we frequently see parties of them. Yesterday I passed a squad under one of their own N.C.O.'s, who gave a smart 'Die Augen – Links!' but the glances from die augen were anything but friendly – poor beggars, I don't blame them; they must have a hard time. The French hate them like poison. I expect we shall have a little more time here before going upstairs again, and that will bring us pretty near the 'offensive' season. However, why worry! I may get off on my signalling course before anything too exciting happens, and that would account for over a month.

We are having a Divisional competition just now for platoons. They have to do a stunt combining some rapid fire and bayonet work, for which various points are given. My platoon is to represent D company, so we have to do a lot of practice; if we win in the Brigade they all get bronze medals, and if in the Division, silver medals. But as the men say, 'What a hope!' However, it's always something to be the best platoon in the company. I've been fostering esprit de platoon by giving prizes [of cigarettes] every time we go on the range for the best scores, and most of the men are quite keen.

Another item in your letter indicates that I had been boasting about freedom from vermin [in a letter of 20 December, 1917, omitted here]. That was a bit premature. I 'got it' immediately thereafter and in fact went home on leave in a pretty lively condition. Aunt Maggie nearly had a fit when the wash lady called her attention to the mobile state of my undergarments. Since coming back I have managed to keep clear of that. I got a bath just after coming out of the trenches, and I can get one here. To do so, however, causes considerable commotion, as the 'madame' regards a bath as a solemn festival not to be lightly undertaken. When I intimated my desire for one, she embarked on a long account of all the officers who had been billeted on her who had had baths, more especially one, a major, who took a cold bath every morning. I don't believe French people ever wash themselves. I've never seen a real bath, 'with taps', in any French house. In fact the old gentleman in the house told me that he thought the English were 'très propre', and that French soldiers would never think of taking a bath unless ordered to do so.

Yesterday evening White and I went into town to see one of the Divisional shows. Of course out here they can do things a little better than when nearer the line; it was an A1 show. The audience contained numerous nurses and 'WAACS' [Women's Auxiliary Army Corps], if you know what that is. It is quite a relief to see any members of the fair sex, after a spell of seeing nothing but muddy soldiers. Of course there are plenty of women here; in fact some of the officers are billeted in a 'chateau' where there is a countess with some charming daughters.

I expect by the time you get this I shall be 'off the duck-boards' again, or further; but perhaps not, and I'm not worrying just now as tonight I shall have a good dinner and a good bed I read a few chapters of *The Way of All Flesh* every night in bed and am enjoying it immensley . . . .

[The 1st Battalion returned to the Passchendaele trenches on 21 February, remaining in tha area until 31 March.]

[Hamburg area]
23 February, 1918

We are up the line again but this time I have 'clicked' for a soft job, being Signals Officer in place of White, who is on leave. I live at Battalion H.Q., which is a pillbox with concrete walls at least six feet thick, and so is pretty safe. The other occupants are the C.O., Adjutant, and Intelligence Officer, and also the doctor (an American) comes in for meals, although he sleeps at the aid post. He is a very decent chap, and well liked. He hails from Utica, N.Y., so we have quite a number of things to talk about. There are two other American doctors at the aid post, one a New Yorker and the other from Cleveland, Ohio. Today I was in for a chat and had a look at a copy of the *Cleveland Plain Dealer*, which contained, inter alia, a 'Krazy Kat' cartoon. So I'm kept in mind of the U.S.A., even in the front line.

Some of these pillboxes are quite good places, although not exactly roomy. Ours has room for a table and chairs, as well as four sleeping bunks along one side, so it is not too bad by any means. Since I would otherwise be living in the posts, I have something to be thankful for this time. My duty is to look after the communications generally, i.e., telephones, lamps, and pigeons. We have a regular signal office with an exchange switchboard and an 'extension' into our quarters; since we came up I have extended the lines right into the front line posts, so it's a pretty complete system. I go round the lines about twice a day and night, visiting all the stations; I also have to see that all the visual (lamp) lines are O.K.'d regularly. It's a very interesting job. The main trouble is shell fire, which sometimes breaks the lines. We have had three or four breaks from that cause in two days. All these pillboxes, by the way, have got names since we got them, and some of these show rather a fine sense of humour. Not far from here there are two, one on each side of the track, one being named 'Cascara Cottage' and the other 'Sagrada Villa'.[32]

Before we left our rest area I managed to bring some kudos to the battalion. I think I told you about the A.R.A. competition that is being held in each Division throughout the B.E.F. My platoon was selected to represent D company. We won successively the Battalion, Brigade, and Divisional rounds, so winning the prize: silver A.R.A medals for each man in the platoon, as well as a money prize. At the final the Divisional Commander was present with his staff and all sorts of brass hats, as well as spectators from the army musketry school; so I acquired some fame. I got personal congratulations from the General Officer Commanding, and also our own Brigadier; and of course the C.O. (who was also there) was highly delighted. The next day he arranged for the platoon to be photographed; he and he Adjutant were in it, so it will be quite an interesting souvenir for me . . . .[33]

['Whitby Camp', near Elverdinghe]
28 February, 1918

When I last wrote you, we were in the line and are now having a few days out prior to the next spasm . . . . Our last few days in the line were pretty lively. There was more activity than usual on both sides, and we had some casualties. On one of my trips round the companies I just happened to arrive as a big strafe started. It was pretty hefty, and S.O.S's were going up all over the shop, which soon produced a fearful noise from our guns, although it lasted only half an hour. On my way down they started shelling the track and I had to bolt for shelter into a small pillbox. I was no sooner inside than a shell landed, wounding two men who were standing just outside – one very badly. I took the other one down to the aid post. He had got a small splinter just above the ear and was spouting blood, but seemed quite happy. Down at the aid post there was another one on a stretcher who had got it in the stomach. He was in a very bad way and kept on shouting, 'Oh God, let me die', and flinging his arms about. It rather gets on one's nerves to listen to that kind of thing, especially in these surroundings. But most of the wounded are very quiet . . . .

['Whitby Camp']
12 March, 1918

On Saturday we went up to the front line again and I was sent to another company which was short of officers. I had four posts to look after and lived in one myself. They were quite decent compared with the last ones I was in, and as the weather was perfect we were quite all right.

Last night I had the biggest piece of luck I've had for some time. After it got dark the company commander came round and warned me that I was to take out a 'fighting patrol' of 20 men and 2 N.C.O.'s, the job being to look for trouble, and to stay out three hours, or until something happened, i.e., until we got a prisoner. I was sitting thinking out the details of this joyful task when another message arrived saying that another officer was taking the patrol, and that I was to proceed down the line toute suite, and report at Divisional H.Q. the following morning for a course in cipher work. It was like waking up from a bad dream. I started off without delay, but had just got off the mark when the Hun started a gas bombardment. It is some job coming down a narrow duckboard track in the dark with a respirator on, and as I had all my equipment and my coat, I was sweating like a pig. The trouble is that every now and then you come to a place where there's a loose board or a board missing, or else a nice watery shell-hole right in the path. At those places you do some sudden and violent gymnastics, which improves your temper. It isn't at all nice when you hear the sound of a shell behind you, and you put on an extra mile per hour, and suddenly fly on your face over a wire. However, I was bound on a good errand, so I didn't mind; but it took me just under two hours to get down to the rear H.Q., where I am living now. This morning I went along to report. There are just three of us – one officer from each Brigade. The class is held in the mess of the Divisional Signals Company from 10 to 12, and will last about four days. We are supposed to do some practice on our own account in the afternoon; but it's the best thing I've struck in months. The O.C. Signals Company told us that the idea is for each Brigade to have an officer trained in cipher work, and that during operations that officer will remain at Brigade H.Q. to look after coding and decoding – which sounds a bit of all right. However, whether that comes off or not, I am in the meantime missing a few days of the line, and getting a fine easy time instead.

During one of the days I was up, the Bosche attacked the people on our left about dawn. They put up the S.O.S. and I've never heard anything like the barrage that came down from our artillery. For an hour every gun in the place was going at it. You can have no idea what it sounded like – it certainly was absolute hell for the Bosche; he was wiped out. One battalion reports 300 dead in front of them; in fact only one man reached our wire. It is really remark-

able how quickly our artillery gets going, and I can tell you it gives
one confidence to hear it. The Bosche artillery is not as good as
ours. He goes in a lot for other things, such as trench mortars and
'minnies'. These are more local in results; but they make a terrific
explosion and they can be very demoralizing. During an S.O.S.
barrage another very noticeable thing is the M.G. fire. The sound
of a large number of machine guns is quite different from the
sound of a single one. It is a kind of wave of sound, quite unbroken,
and also very capable of 'getting the wind up' anyone in front.
Although it's unpleasant to be in the front line during these perfor-
mances, it is great to see the shells bursting all along the Bosche
line. As an exhibition of fireworks it takes some beating –
especially as Fritz adds to it by a liberal use of signal rockets, star
shells, and so forth. He is great on these; one would think sometimes that every man had a supply, because on one occasion I
recall when his trench mortars started firing they were dropping
into his own posts, and at once red lights (the signal, evidently, to
lengthen range) went popping up all over the place. On our side we
hardly ever put up a light. I expect that's one reason he does it so
much, because he never knows what we're up to, whereas when
he's shooting lights up in No Man's Land we have a fair idea that
none of his patrols are out at the time . . . .

['Crest Farm' trenches, Passchendaele]
23 March, 1918

I am writing this from my front line post so you will excuse
paper, writing, etc. I received the *Radiator* (with your article on
Soldiers' Insurance), and also the *Literary Digest*. The latter is the
sole piece of reading matter I have had up here, and at the present
moment my corporal is reading it. Just now I notice he is at the
page devoted to 'Current Poetry', which you might think rather
funny, if you knew him.

I got rather a shock when I came up to take over, as I found that
the post I am in charge of was a new one (pushed forward of
course); the accommodation I found for myself and eight men was
a hole about six yards long and two feet deep, with about a foot of
water in it. The men didn't half use some expressive language. But
we got started working, and now after two nights we've made it into
quite a decent place, about five feet deep, and with sides revetted
and floor boards in, and a small shelter at each end. The trench fell
in about three times during the work, causing a great flow of
blasphemy. But we are used to such discouragement. All the

ground here is so shaken up with explosions that it will hardly hold together without support.

I have only the one post this time, so I could pick the best men from my platoon. They are a pretty tough lot, and I honestly believe some of them are quite sorry when the night passes without something more exciting than usual. For instance, last night the sentry thought he saw something in front, and we had to stand to; but fortunately (to my mind) it was a false alarm. But when I gave the order to stand down one of the men said regretfully, 'I thought we was going to have a bit of sport that time, sir', and I had to pretend I was frightfully sorry we hadn't been raided or something equally nice. As a matter of fact we are in a fairly good position, as the ground in front is nothing but waterlogged shell-holes, and we got out a little wire last night pretty nearly all round the post. As it is moonlight just now it would be difficult for Fritz to get up to us without being seen. If we do see him first we can give him something, as besides rifles we have a Lewis gun and plenty of bombs. So far, however, I don't think he knows we're here, as we cover the place during the day with camouflage; at present all his stuff is going right over us.

I'm occupying one of the small shelters with my servant; it is just big enough for us to get in, and he has to do the cooking outside. This morning my breakfast was café au lait (tinned), bacon and sausage, bread and marmalade, which is pretty good going in a place like this. Breakfast is the best meal of the day. For dinner we have to fall back on bully-beef, while tea is generally tea, bread and jam, or cheese, perhaps with sardines or something like that. Of course everything is more or less filthy. But one gets used to that, and I guess I've eaten my 'peck of dirt' a few times. During the night the men get stew and tea, which is brought up in 'hot food containers', and also rum, and I take a share of each – and the last is not the least. Although the stew is A1 stuff, the men prefer the tea and rum, as is evident from their remarks when they hear which it is; and that seems rather funny, as the stew is the principal meal they get. During the day they make tea for themselves, or (as it's called) 'drum up', and with that they have their other rations: bread, jam, etc.

> *[On 21 March the Germans opened an offensive, initially directed against British forces south of the river Scarpe, thrusting through Bapaume and Peronne. On 31 March the 33rd Division was concentrated west of Arras, to assist if called upon*

*in checking the German advance. When this
phase of the enemy effort was halted, on the
general line Beaumont Hamel-Albert-Villers
Bretonneux-Montdidier (without involving the
33rd Division), a re-directed German push on 9
April attacked British positions north and south
of the river Lys, breaking the line between
Givenchy and Laventie. In response, on 10 April,
the 33rd Division entrained for Caestre; by late
afternoon the following day the 1st Battalion and
other elements of the 19th Brigade had occupied
positions in the Meteren area, to check a German
advance toward Bailleul and Hazebrouck. Thereafter, until 21 April, the 19th Brigade played a
major role in the confused and desperate fighting
around Meteren and Merris that at length frus-
trated German efforts to break through to the
high ground beyond, from Mt. Kemmel to Mont
des Cats.]*

[Brandhoek]
29 March, 1918

We get a few days here and then back [into the line] again; but it
is quite possible, and I believe probable, that we may be pushed off
south into the big battle. Meantime all leave and schools are
stopped, and our rest, which was just due, is 'napoo' [i.e., finished,
dead]. The Bosche certainly did some push, all right, but latest
news is that he is now held, and a little bit more. I think the situation is not so bad now.

We had a two-hour trip in open trucks down here, and as it was
freezing we were pretty cold by the time we got in (12:30 a.m.). But
there was a good fire and a good dinner waiting, and reveille next
morning was at 10; so we soon forgot our troubles. I was commanding D company for the last three days in the line, as Craig got
slightly wounded while going round with the C.O.; but he is back
again. While down here we do fatigues. This afternoon I have to
take a party to load ten trucks with bricks. These have first to be
excavated from the surrounding ruins; as you see, 'rest' is an elastic
term. We got a new C.O. a few days ago – Lt.-Col. Draffen, D.S.O.
from the 2nd Battalion.[34] He seems a fine chap, but is très
moutarde, and has everybody 'tied to the mast and begging for
mercy' already. By the way, Cole was interested in your remarks

137

about Henri Verbrugghen, whom he knows very well. He has just had to send his violin home, as just now we have all got to get our kits down to the minimum, in view of possible quick moves.

I had a letter from Mr. Moir, and also a copy of *Harper's* and *The Economic World*. I wrote him a long letter in reply. I'm glad to hear that you are finding life in Springfield and conditions in general congenial . . . .

[Brandhoek]
30 March, 1918

Although I just wrote a few days ago, I write again as I have since received yours of 13 March, and also packets of papers. Tonight two or three of the other officers, including the Doc (a Canadian), were in our mess and in a few minutes they were all sitting reading your papers. So they are appreciated, all right. I received also a further paper from Mr. Moir. It's very good to see that he is keeping me so much in mind . . . Sending parcels from your end seems to be a very risky proceeding. If I should want anything very badly I can write to Uncle Rod and tell him that you will settle up, but at present I am all right. I shall be very glad to receive the socks from Amy though, and feel honoured to get her first pair. We have to change socks daily when in the line and of course the officers don't get an issue, as the men do.

By the way, may I cancel sufficient of the above to ask you to send me a copy of *Barrack Room Ballads*, including if possible the other poems. It's no use sending an expensive copy, as it won't survive the treatment it gets here; so the cheapest one available is the thing. The only 'civilian' book I carry about is *The Oxford Book of English Verse*. But when going into the line I generally try to get a magazine or two, and sometimes they survive when we are up, which is the best way.

I don't know that I have much news. As regards the battle, you will by the time this reaches you know a lot more than I do now, so it's not much use saying anything, except that from our latest news the situation seems to be much improved and getting into hand again. Evidently we are not for it, meantime; at the moment we are still out of the immediate front, and we are doing working parties. Yesterday Brodie (C company) was killed, and Clay, among others, wounded by a stray shell.[35] Brodie was one of the best, and his death has given us all a bit of a knock. He is being buried here tomorrow. The men who were killed at the same time as Brodie were buried up there today without the services of a padre, but there's sure to be one on deck tomorrow to do a little spectacular work in a comparatively safe place. My experience is that the padre who comes into the danger zone is a 'rara avis'. Our battalion padre happens to be the R.C. one. He is about 25, but he expects all the R.C.'s in the battalion to call him 'Father'.

I hadn't such a bad birthday today. The programme was 8:30 a.m. to 5 p.m., with working party on the Divisional reserve line. We travelled each way by light railway. On the way back it was raining like the dickens and I had no coat; but I got a seat in the cab of the engine and kept dry. I had 'lunch' at 5:30 and dinner at 8:30, and am writing this before hitting the hay. Uncle Rod sent me a parcel, containing a cake (made by Aunt Maggie – very good), a box of biscuits, a Veda Loaf[36], and chocolates; the latter, being opened in the mess, lasted about ten seconds.

[Grand Rullecourt]
9 April, 1918

. . . Our first billet in this area was a huge chateau in beautiful grounds, and it was 'the goods' if we could only have stayed there for a bit; but of course we didn't. At the moment we are in a very one-horse little village. The interpreter got me a billet in which he said there was a bed. When I arrived about 10 p.m. I found two excessively filthy mattresses, which consituted the entire bedding. I summoned Madame and demanded sheets; after much argument she agreed, returning with the sheets which she held out to me, saying, 'Voilà M'sieur'. I explained that I wanted them put on the bed, and when the idea sunk in she laid them on the bed as they were and made for the door once more. It took another five minutes to persuade her to make the bed, but I did get it done at last.

Just now all leave is stopped, so my special leave[37] is hung up. The situation seems more settled now, and I believe our 'heid yins' ['brass hats'; military commanders] are pretty well satisfied. But there may be plenty of dirty work yet. All courses are stopped too; there was an inquiry recently for officers with special qualifications of any sort and my name was sent in, but whether anything will come of it is very doubtful. Thanks for offering to buy cigarettes for my platoon, but there are so many changes already that I don't think I will do anything more in that line. I have a fine big platoon now – 56 all told, and generally over 40 on parade. I've had the same platoon longer than any officer in the battalion now, so I'm developing into an old soldier . . . .

[Mont des Cats]
18 April, 1918

I don't know when I'll get this letter off, but a brief respite in the battle gives me an opportunity of writing, of which I'd better take advantage. During the last nine days we have been having it hot and strong, and I've seen enough of the war to do me some time.[38] As you know, of course, the Bosche has been making some big efforts to break through lately, so we have pretty well been up against it. I can't go into details of places (of course), but a rough summary of what I've been doing for the past week or two will give you an idea of what kind of time we've had.

The first thing was that we got notice at 9 p.m. one night [10 April] that we had to prepare to move at once. We marched about 10 miles to a place where we were to entrain [Aubigny], arriving at about 2 a.m., and slept on the street until 6 a.m. when we got on the train. We had an eight-hour journey, during which our diet was chocolate and biscuits; on arrival we marched four miles to where we were to stay the night. There were no billets and we slept in the open, but the weather was all right so it was not bad, especially as we were all dog-tired. On our way up we passed streams of refugees. It was a sad sight to see some of them – especially the old men and women being helped along the road. Next day the Bosche had got his guns on the place where we were, and before long the village was being knocked about to some tune, several houses being set on fire. That morning I got the joyful news that Craig was to be kept among the reserve of officers, and that I would take the company into action, my other officers being Roger, Anderson, and Cole.[39] I didn't get orders until the evening, when I was given a map reference of a place about three kilometres away, and told to take the company and dig ourselves in on that line. Of course it was dark when we got up, and I can tell you I had some job, as the country is quite 'close', i.e., fields of crops, etc., but we got it done somehow, and linked up with other troops on our left and right. There was a small farm just behind us, so I established company H.Q. there. I found the farm about 3 a.m.; when I went in there were two or three old women and some children still there, all limp with terror. I induced them to clear out next morning, which they did, leaving everything as it was – cows, hens, etc., all over the place. It was just as well they did go, as the farm was shelled next day; but we hung on to it as there was a good cellar.

Next day there were attacks on our left, and a bit of a demonstration in front, and I had to send reinforcements to other companies two or three times. The Bosche was close up; the whole time both sides were sniping and machine-gunning like the dickens. That afternoon Cole was killed, along with his servant. He had gone in to a little bit of a shack to get some food, and a shell landed plump on the roof. It set the place on fire; when we did get Cole's body next day it was burnt to a cinder. We did four nights up there and had a lively time. But on our section the whole line held; and I believe G.H.Q. has sent congratulations to our Brigade. I sniped a Bosche one morning myself. I was in the front line at the time, and saw him put his head up, about 100 yards off. I waited and the next time got him, as we saw him go backwards. But the men were getting them all the time. Anderson was wounded the second day, leaving me with only one other officer. We had some prisoners brought in by our patrols; one of them was an N.C.O. who could speak French, so I examined him and got a lot of interesting information about the strength and disposition of the troops opposite. Incidentally he told us that they were going to attack next morning, which they did; but more to my left, and as they were beaten off all right I wasn't involved.

The fourth night we were relieved, and marched back a short distance, arriving at our billet [Fontaine Houch] about 4 a.m. – only to be told that there was a threatened attack at another point, and that we had to put out outposts and prepare to move at short notice. If you could realise how tired the men were you would have an idea of what that meant to us; but there was nothing for it. We got orders to move again at 10 a.m., and once more found ourselves manning a line, under terrific shell fire. But they only kept us up about 24 hours, as some fresh troops came up to counter-attack, and we were again taken back. It was only a short march, but the men were so tired that it was simply a stagger all the way. When we did get to the place where we were supposed to get billets, we found them full of French cavalry, and were told we would have to squat on the road. However, D company officers had a scout round, and we found a small brewery all locked up – but we broke in the door and got all the men in there. For ourselves we found a small cottage which had been left with everything intact, beds, furniture, crockery, *and* hens. We didn't half have an American Sunday dinner. We've now had a whole night there; I had my first night's sleep in eight days. But what we'll be doing next I don't know; we get no news, although the rumour is that the Bosche is retiring again. Just now we live like fighting cocks, as there are pigs, hens, potatoes, eggs, etc., and plenty of wine. We have six bottles of white wine in our cottage, and one of the other companies found a case of champagne. Of course, we can buy nothing, so that either we live entirely on rations (my last day in the line I had one slice of bread, two pieces of bacon, and a drink of water), or else we are in some place such as this where we find supplies of all sorts lying about . . . .

I'm in A1 condition, except for sore feet, having had my boots on continuously for over a week. I hadn't a change of socks with me, as we were rushed off in such a hurry that I had hardly time to get anything; and as I was out in wet ground I got my feet soaking wet, and they've been like that practically the whole time. I hope things will quiet down a bit soon, as we've had enough of it. But I think the Bosche has had 'encore de plus' [more than enough]. The prisoners we took told us they had been in for six days, and were about starving, to say nothing of being wet and miserable. One N.C.O. asked me if he would be shot; I told him probably not, and he added, 'Je suis fiancé'. Poor devil, he had the wind up badly . . . .

[Ste. Marie Cappel, SE of Cassel]
24 April, 1918

I think I wrote you last when we were enjoying a brief respite. It was brief, all right; after one night there we got orders to move up into reserve again.[40] We left at 4 a.m. and got into position about 6, in open fields, where we lay all day. As it rained, snowed, and hailed, it wasn't very pleasant – to say nothing of the shelling, which was pretty hot. So we were glad when we got orders that evening to move up to the front line. We only did . . . [CENSORED] . . . the men were pretty well used up by that time and it was comparatively quiet. Our relief turned up at 2 a.m. next morning, and we came back here, where we are having something more like a proper rest.

My feet were very bad on account of having my boots on for about ten days, and wet feet most of the time. When we reached our halting place for breakfast I was absolutely crocked, and could go no further. Goble[41] was likewise, so when the battalion continued the march we were left behind in charge of the lame and lazy. We were there the whole day, and as we had no rations we did a bit of foraging; we got a good fire going in a deserted estaminet, and having found a couple of tins of army rations and some butter we got potatoes out of a field and had an A1 dinner. We were picked up eventually about 10 p.m. by some ambulances and taken on here. I've been on the sick list since, but will be all right soon. This is a very fine camp. It is away from shell-fire; we get bombed occasionally but of course that is all in the day's work.

Canadian troops carry 'trench mats' (duckboards) in a ravaged landscape.

2nd Lieutenant Herbert W. Cole, 'one of the finest fellows I ever knew'. He was killed in action on 14 April, 1918, near Meteren.

I don't know if I told you that two of the officers who were in the 6th with me at home – Thorburn and Loudon – came out here about two weeks ago and were killed in this last show[42]; and another – Wilson – was wounded. Rather a brief career for them, poor beggars. Some people don't last very long.

So far as I know the situation here is much better now. For the last week or more our artillery and the French artillery have been giving the Bosche gyp [a rough time] in his new positions. In some places it must be absolute hell for him. The French '75s' are marvellous for rapid artillery fire. They keep going all the time. I suppose that in due course there will be some big counter-attacks, but as yet we are still staving off the push – and pretty effectively, I think.

[Ste. Marie Cappel]
25 April, 1918

[From a letter to Amy Maclean] ... It was very sad to see all these little houses and farms, which had been occupied so recently, going to ruin, and in some cases being set on fire by German shells. It brought home the horrors of war to us more than many other things. I wonder how some of our people at home would stand that sort of thing. We had a good many casualties in our company, including Mr. Cole, who had only recently come out. He was married only about a week before. I am sure it will be a great shock to his wife. He was one of the finest fellows I ever knew, and a great musician . . . .

[Maclean was sent to hospital in Boulogne, ('with such a plebian complaint as boils, and miscellaneous swellings on my head') on 3 May; he returned to 'B Echelon' on 17 May, rejoining the main body of the battalion on 19 May, when he took command of B company. Meanwhile, on 3 May the 1st Battalion moved to the Poperinghe area, and two days later to the vicinity of Busseboom, with D company holding an advanced position at Ouderdom. When a German attack on 8 May drove French and British troops back from the Kemmel Beek, the 1st Battalion moved up to Hallebast and attacked that evening across the Kemmel Beek (with the 5/6 Scottish

Rifles, and French troops) in an attempt to recover
the lost ground; but the attack was a costly failure.
The 1st Battalion suffered heavily; according to the
Battalion War Diary, there were 'only about 80
men left' after the battle. Lt.-Col. Draffen was
badly wounded, and taken prisoner. On 21 may
Lt.-Col. G. Wingate, a Territorial officer, took
command of the 1st Battalion.]

[Elverdinghe, NW of Poperinghe]
19 May, 1918

I wrote you a couple of days ago after arriving at B Echelon. We got orders to remain there, and the battalion came out next morning – much altered – we are now in camp about seven miles back and will I think go further back. One result of the losses, among officers, is that I have been posted to command B company. This might mean in the course of some weeks that I would get the acting rank (and pay) of Captain; and as they haven't many other officers available for the job I may not get hoofed out before that happens – but it may not happen at all. However, in the meantime I enjoy the privileges of the job, including a horse.

I got more details of the current operations, and our battalion certainly had a rough time. They were detailed to make a feint attack to attract the attention of the enemy, while the rest of the Brigade sneaked up and delivered one in the solar plexus, and were successful in doing so. But of course they got machine-gunned and shelled to blazes. And I certainly was lucky to be elsewhere. Tomorrow we are being inspected by General Plumer[43], and I expect will get a few kind words. But no doubt his real object is to see if we're fit for any more dirty work just at present.

I received your letter of April 24th, with enclosures, today; and I note that you have sent a copy of *Barrack Room Ballads*, for which many thanks. I was interested in the programme of your dinner, although your subject does not strike me as one calculated to arouse much enthusiasm at a banquet. However, no doubt your eloquence 'put it across'. Here we are all scrubbing up for General P., and the scene is peaceful, although we can see German shells bursting on the ridge in front, and hear our own doing their little bit. But back here it is a case of 'we should worry' – although he does send a long distance one (or 'whistling Percy') now and then.

[Brandhoek area]
26 May, 1918

The copy of *Barrack Room Ballads* arrived today, for which many thanks. It is a very nice copy, and in spite of limitations on the size of officers' kit I shall add it to mine. We are only allowed 58 lbs. gross weight, and lately they've been very strict about this; and as there are certain indispensables such as 'flea-bag', blanket, spare clothes and boots – to say nothing of the weight of the valise itself –there isn't much margin for luxuries . . . .

We are still pretty well back and at present are doing working parties on some of the new trenches. We parade at 4:30 every morning, so you can see I'm leading the simple life. We finish before 10 a.m., however, and have most of the remainder of the day free. I am still flourishing, more or less, as O.C. B company. The other officers in the company are all right; we have a very jovial mess. One of the 'subs' is an old ranker, a right tough specimen, and his tales of life in the 1st Cameronians are très amusing. He has the Military Medal and Mons Star – quite a useful person. One of the others –Chambers – was in the ranks of the 1st Cameronians at the beginning of the war and has been three times wounded; so I have some support.[44]

P.S. Army slang for very salt bacon – 'a bit of Lot's wife'.[45]

[Brandhoek]
30 May, 1918

. . . We are not in the line yet but fairly close up, and getting some shelling. Our little house has escaped so far, but there are shell holes all round it, the closest being about 30 yards, and we are more or less living in expectation. Of course, if he lands one very close we clear out toute suite. In fact I have had to clear one platoon out of its billets already. The Adjutant told me today that I am one of the two company commanders who are to remain out this time, so when the battalion goes I shall be going back to B Echelon. I also heard that leave had opened again. These two events in conjunction have caused me to re-submit my application for special leave, which I did today. I've applied for June 12-26, so that if it is granted I shall very probably be an old married man before you get this. But of course if everything comes off all right I shall cable you the glad tidings.[46] I say 'very probably' because many things may happen to bust it up, and I shall not feel by any means certain of it until I am well clear, and even then there will be difficulties at the other end. If anything does happen to stop it, it will be pretty awkward, as Marjorie will have to start off within a few days of getting the wire I sent today, and I shall not hear whether the leave is granted or not until within a day or two of the actual date of departure . . . . I hope this new German offensive doesn't cause all leave to be hung up again but our latest news as I write is more reassuring. By the way I believe there is some possibility of my being made signalling officer. When Major Hunter and Wigan [47]come back I can't very well be left with a company, and as White is probably becoming Assistant Adjutant I spoke to the C.O. today about it, and he is going to let me know. I hope it comes off as, comparatively speaking, it is a bon job . . . .

[B Echelon, W of Poperinghe]
7 June, 1918

I just got word last night that my leave has been approved by Army H.Q., so by the time you get this I expect to have done the deed. The leave is for June 12-26, and I am getting away on the 10th, as just now we are well in the wilds, and I expect it will take a couple of days at least to get Paris. I have to do several miles to railhead, where I get the 'daily personnel train' which moves by bounds of about 100 yards at a time, and goes round in circles; so it takes some considerable time to get to a town where I can get a 'civilian' train for Paris. But I expect I'll manage Bordeaux by the 13th. I got a wire off to Spain to give them four days or so to get up. I shall cable you when the glad event takes place, so you'll know about it before this reaches you.

I'm having an easy time just now, at B Echelon with the reserves. We have an A1 little camp with a Nissen hut for our mess. I'm doing mess president and we do ourselves well – we managed a bottle of Benedictine last night, and H.Q. left us a dozen of port, so we were able to celebrate my good luck. The O.C. Echelon is Capt. [R.F.R.] Becher, formerly our Adjutant. He is a 'pukka' regular, an Irishman, and a very nice fellow; we get on very well. He's made me adjutant of the echelon, but there is little to do except write formal orders. I have my horse here, so I can get a ride whenever I want. During the day the weather is too warm for that, but before breakfast and in the evening it is 'the business' – as the Glasgow Keelies say. I regret that I can't confirm the report of my having been made Captain, although if I manage to hang on to B company I should get it ultimately. The difference in pay is only 2/-, but of course the rank counts for a lot. The signalling job is off now (White has taken it on again); but of course if I get a company permanently I should prefer it.

Just now I have another job – escort to our chaplain, who is under arrest. He is an Irish R.C., and his crime was refusing to attend church parade when General Plumer inspected us. However, as there's nowhere for him to run away to I don't bother much about him.

Paris
20 June, 1918

I expect you have received my cable with the information that Marjorie and I were duly married yesterday. After many difficulties we managed to fix it up; the wedding took place, both at the Consulate and at the Scottish Church in Paris afterwards, by a padre with the good old Scotch name of Kesting. 'Those present' were Aunt Jessie, Mr. and Mrs. D.L.S. Douglas, and Mr. and Mrs. Dickson; you will remember Dickson as a former friend of yours at the High School.[48] Afterwards we came back to the hotel for a very nice luncheon; everything went off in good style. I was very glad for Marjorie's sake that we managed the church marriage, and also could rake up a few friends, as it made a little more of it than the strictly business transaction which it would otherwise have been. We're going to spend the remainder of my leave in Paris, and will be there until the 27th, with a possible extension of leave for seven days (in view of the delay caused by going to Bordeaux).

Paris is O.K. for a holiday. Last night Marjorie and I went to a show, and had dinner at Paillard's, on the Boulevard des Capucines, one of the best places. Tonight or tomorrow we are going to the Grand Guignol, and we'll also 'take in' the Opéra Comique. Before Marjorie came I went to one of the music halls, but I certainly shall not take any ladies there. They had one sketch that was really too awful; but some of the others were A1. Things are of course very dear, but I'm allowing myself a bit of extravagance this trip. We have a fine room at the hotel [the Palais d'Orsay], with bath; and a good view of Paris and the Seine from our window. It's well worth the charge of 25 francs per diem. I'm getting to know my way about a bit now, and can buzz around on the Métro like an old-timer. Taxis are cheap, so there is no difficulty in getting around. The shops and streets are beautiful; hours can be spent just strolling along such streets as the Rue de

Rivoli, Avenue de l'Opéra, and all the boulevards. Weather is warm and fine. Things are at their best just now in the Bois and in the Tuileries Gardens (just across the street from the hotel); there is a great show of roses and other flowers.

[From a letter of 1 July] The pleasantest way of passing the evening was a stroll round, as the weather was ideal, and everything round about the hotel is lovely – Tuileries Gardens, Champs Elysées, along the Seine – we always did that after dinner. The Palais d'Orsay is a top-hole hotel. In fact it was all too good to last. But at any rate I've no regrets. I don't think I could have had a better time anywhere.

[Maclean returned to the 1st Battalion on 3 July. While he was on leave, the battalion occupied trenches in the Dickebusch area, suffering 126 casualties during the 'quiet' month of June. On 19 July Major (later Brigadier-General) James Jack, D.S.O., who had served with both regular battalions of The Cameronians in 1914-1916, and who commanded the 2nd West Yorkshires from August, 1916 until July, 1917, assumed command of the 1st Battalion. He continued as C.O. until 7 September, when he was appointed to command the 28th Infantry Brigade, 9th (Scottish) Division.]

[Voormezeele trenches, Ypres Canal]
25 July, 1918

I was very pleased to receive your letter of 3 July tonight. We are up the line at present and although at the moment my company is not in the front line I am having a fairly worrying time, as things are pretty lively on this front and an attack is not impossible. A couple of months ago there were rumours of one, and we were detailed to do a counter-attack in case the Bosche broke the front line. My blokes were all standing-to all night, awaiting orders, and I had the breeze up, more or less. One's peace of mind is not helped on these occasions by the violent spasms of our artillery, which they indulge in as 'counter-preparation' fire when they think Fritz is coming across. We certainly gave him something that night, and his coloured lights were going up like 'billy-oh'. Ultimately nothing happened, but it's a bit of a strain nonetheless.

Just now I have an American officer with B company[49], and as my company H.Q. (which is a pretty roomy place) is also used by some machine gun people, who also have Americans, it is quite like being at home again. They all come from North Carolina, and it is fine to hear their Southern accent. They are an A1 bunch, as keen as possible. It is certainly a pleasure to show them around. They want to see everything and do everything. Tonight my American is out voluntarily on a carrying party with one of my subs. He will be out until about 2 a.m. and will have to go over some very dangerous ground; but he was anxious to go, just the same. One of the other 'Yanks' is a bit of a humorist. Today he was describing for my benefit a Southern game, 'crap-shooting', and it was as good as Bert Williams [the first black to be featured in American musical comedy].

I don't remember if I told you that we have a new commanding officer – Major Jack (D.S.O. and Legion of Honour). He is what we call a 'pukka soldier', i.e., a regular; and he belongs to the 1st Battalion, having come out with them in 1914. He has got hot and strong ideas on the subject of discipline, which are making everyone sit up. Fortunately I seem to have made a reasonably good impression, as he told me yesterday that he was very satisfied with B company – much to my relief, as I wouldn't have gathered it from his observations on his way round the company. He is a fine-looking chap, tall and thin, with a fine string of ribbons on his chest – a regular live wire.

[Vlamertinghe, W of Ypres]
2 August, 1918

At present we are having a few days' rest between spells in the line, but are only a few miles back and not in the 'shopping zone'. My H.Q. is the usual ruined farm; in good weather it is O.K. but when, as today, it is raining the rain comes in everywhere. But we have beds, of sorts, and our valises, and we can get a fairly decent night's sleep, and more or less decent meals, so it's all right. B company was reserve last time so we're for the front line next trip, which will be the first time I've commanded a company in the front line, except the few days in April when we had the Bosche attack to hold up. Fortunately I've managed to make a good impression on the new Commanding Officer. Last time up he told me he was very satisfied with 'the way I did things'. Later on he invited me to dinner at the H.Q. mess, and was very decent; so I am in pretty soft just at present. He is a top-hole Colonel, and we should do all right with him. He was speaking about my Captaincy, and I believe there is a fair chance of my getting it. The difficulty, however, is that there are so many of that rank who are nominally on strength of the 1st Battalion although not with the unit. It is quite all right being a Company Commander while out of the line, as I get various privileges, but I could do with the pay as well. I think I told you that our new Second-in-Command is an 'honourable', and the son of a former Chancellor of the Exchequer[50]; so we are well looked after.

I am keeping in first rate form just now, and wouldn't mind a tour up front, if the weather would only clear up; but when it is wet there it is pure misery for everyone – especially the poor wretches of men, some of whom don't even have head cover. We don't take overcoats up in summertime, so the only protection they have is a waterproof sheet. I think every one of those fellows deserves a medal. But of course they don't get it.

I had a very fine American officer up with me last time, a fellow named Bellamy, from North Carolina. I believe his father is a millionaire cotton man; in any event he has a fine son. The men were also A1, and as keen as anything.

[Support trenches, Ypres Canal]
9 August, 1918

We are up in the line again. My company has been in support but goes into the front line again tonight. My H.Q. for the last few days has been in the cellar of what used to be a chateau. The chateau however is now represented by a mass of bricks and stones – which provide excellent cover, and protection against shells, so far as the cellar is concerned, as it's all piled up on top, so that it would take some shell to go through the lot. A Company Commander's job in the line is no cinch, I can assure you. I can scarcely manage two hours' consecutive sleep, and generally don't get more than four out of twenty-four. Then there are the visits of the C.O., the Brigadier, and so forth, who come at the most ungodly hours, and always have umpteen criticisms to make. On the other hand our doc has his aid post down here too (there is quite a series of subterranean apartments), and we have our grub together, which is very pleasant, as he is an exceptionally nice fellow. There's also the advantage that as he is a member of Battalion H.Q. his 'extra rations' are O.K. – we have some really decent meals.

Meteren, September 1918.

What once was Passchendaele.

This afternoon we had our firework display as our guns had a 'concentration' on a part of the enemy defences just opposite. It looked as if the whole place was on fire; the bursts of smoke thrown up by the shells were practically continuous, and any unlucky Bosche who happened to be there must have had a devil of a time.... We have excellent news from the south today[51], and I think the Bosche must be beginning to feel slightly worried ....

[Front line trenches, Ypres Canal]
13 August, 1918

Last night I got your letter of July 18. I can assure you your letters are always welcome and interesting, especially when up here. Last night I got seven letters, and a parcel from Mrs. Cole, so I am not forgotten. I note what you say about tobacco and shall be glad to receive some of your own brand. I have been living on ration tobacco lately so far as pipe-smoking is concerned. It is not A1 stuff, but is always a smoke, and there's plenty of it. Besides your 'fags', Marjorie sent me 100 the other day, and some unknown benefactor sent three tins of Gold Flake, so I have plenty just now.

I'm in the front line at present. The weather is warm and conditions are good. Unfortunately in this area warm weather means smells, so it isn't all 'lavender'. My company H.Q. is quite a decent little place (concreted) on the bank of a well-known canal, into which Jerry drops a few shells, 'minnies', etc., every day, and down which he fires his M.G.'s at night; but it is really quite a good spot. I've had many a worse place. Last night it was converted into a sort of advanced aid post, as one of my patrols got in touch with the Bosche and we had half a dozen or so casualties.[52] Some of them were sick and all very muddy and bloody, and in a small place like that on a warm night the atmosphere was 'a bit thick'. One of my officers who was with them got a chunk from a rifle grenade in his leg. It was some job getting him carried out and put on the stretcher. We had to cut the leg off his breeches to get at the wound as he was a bit of a sight, but (as we say) he was 'laughing', i.e., he had a good 'Blighty' one, so he stuck it all right. I had a very narrow escape myself the other morning when I was going round the posts just before dawn. The Bosche suddenly put down an intense barrage of 'whiz-bangs' on the front line. I had to run like blazes to get into the next post (a section of trench about 20 yards long), and got there only to find that that was right in the middle of the show.

One shell came right in, killing two men not a couple of yards from me. I certainly had the wind up properly. One of the men who was killed went down partly on a stretcher and the remainder in two sandbags, which shows what a lovely war it is – I don't think.

I'm very well off for reading matter, what with your magazines and some stuff left by previous occupants. There is a copy of Conan Doyle's *The Refugees*, which I have much enjoyed. Another good point about this place is that there is a Corps trench wireless close by and the operator sends me in the Paris Press news every afternoon. The news is top-hole these days, and the German people must be thinking furiously. I believe that to date some 1200 guns and 33,000 prisoners have been taken since July 15, and ground won in the most useful places. In fact, I think it is good enough to have real influence on the duration of the war. I hope and expect that still more good news is to come.

I am keeping very fit just now, but after four or five days here am pretty tired, as I can't manage more than three or four hours sleep a day on account of duties and calls to the telephone, etc. Just now a bed and 12 hours to stay in it would look good to me. The worst time is between one and four a.m. – unless I'm on the move I have to keep wakening myself up all the time. We don't sleep at all at night in the front line, but of course just now nights are very short. B company was to have done a raid this trip, but I got word last night that it was off – some relief!

[La Commune, Licques, E of Boulogne]
24 August, 1918

At present I am on holiday, in a sense – the battalion is out for a rest and we are in a very peaceful little town miles from the front. My company is by itself in a sort of suburb, and we have an A1 little cottage for our mess, with a beautiful garden at the back containing fruit-trees, flowers, beehives; altogether a charming place. The weather is warm and we've been having meals outside; it is top-hole. We work from 7 a.m. to 12 or thereabouts; but I have about a million things to attend to every day, so I haven't had much spare time so far.

You will be glad to hear that the papers for my promotion to Captain have been sent in; I expect it will be through shortly. The C.O. has been very affable and complimentary lately, and I get on well with him in spite of his eccentricities. You would enjoy listening to him talk, as he is in some ways a typical 'regular' – and most amusing. He carries a hunting horn on parade and uses it instead of a whistle, much to the men's amusement, but he is hot stuff all the same, and as brave as a lion; so we can put up with other things. The following instance will give you an idea of the sort of thing he does. Some of my men were doing musketry, standing at the foot of a high bank. The C.O. told me quietly to send a man up to the top, who was suddenly to throw a huge clod of earth into the middle of the musketry crowd. When this was done he yelled out, 'Enemy bomber!' – the idea being to see what the men would do. I thought they would die laughing. But fortunately they rose to the occasion and promptly shot the bomber.

You say I will be surprised to find how many 'Yanks' are over here, but I don't know about that – I've seen a great many of them and met quite a lot. They are all right, although they have different ideas from us on some things. It is rather funny to us, for instance, to see an officer's servant walk in and sit down, and even ask his officer if he can oblige with a cigarette. If one of ours did that I suppose he would be dragged out and shot forthwith, unless the officer dropped dead from shock. However, these are minor matters as regards winning the war, and I'm quite sure the American army is going to do a good share of that.

News still keeps good; every day we hear of more places captured and more prisoners taken; and although there's been nothing for a while, all these things mount up. They give the impression that the Bosche is staggering. He won't admit it for a while yet, I'm afraid . . . .

[La Commune, Licques]
26 August, 1918

Our much-longed-for rest has been nipped in the bud, and we have orders to move tomorrow, but don't know yet where we are going. I shouldn't be surprised if we went down south to help battle the Bosche back, and I hope that's what it is, but of course I can't say. This may and probably does mean that our push is succeeding well beyond expectations; certainly the news these days is O.K. I hear today that Bapaume is retaken. We seem to be going ahead somewhere all the time, so it would be all right to get into that. On the other hand, if we are just going back to our old haunts we shall feel pretty fed up . . . .

[The 1st Battalion moved on 28-29 August to Ivergny, NE of Doullens, for two weeks of training. Maclean was hospitalized in Boulogne with

*influenza on 3 September; he rejoined the
'minimum reserve' of the battalion on 30 September. Meanwhile the 1st Battalion moved on 14
September to Etricourt, as part of the larger
movement of the 33rd Division, now part of V
Corps, Third Army. On 21 September, unsuppor-
ted by tanks and with slight artillery preparation,
the 1st Battalion attacked German positions
covering a sunken road ('Gloucester Road') near
Villers Guislain; but this thrust, during which the
battalion suffered heavy casualties, was unsuccessful. After the battle only Lt. J.C. Kerr and one
other officer remained to collect survivors.]*

[Beaulencourt, SE of Bapaume]
1 October, 1918

I have returned to the battalion now – or rather to 'C Echelon',
which is the reserve portion while the battalion is in the line, as it is
now; and I have instructions to remain there meantime, as C.O.
Echelon. I got a huge mail when I got back, including a consign-
ment of cigarettes, several packets of papers, and four letters from
you – the total was about 30, but I needn't say where most of these
came from [i.e., from Marjorie Maclean]. I had a very long and
weary journey back and am now in an area totally new to me, but
which is very famous in the war; the name of every village would
be familiar to you. Signs of the recent Bosche occupation abound
on every side, and everything in the nature of a building is
obliterated. It is interesting to see all the signboards in German,
and to think that they were put up only a few months ago by a victorious army – which now 'has its skates on' and is travelling in the
opposite direction.

Accommodation is primitive; as O.C. I have a magnificent 6' ×
4' shack with ample ventilation. Yesterday the whole rear outfit
moved forward about 5 miles, which shows how things are going. I
expect I shall be going up front soon, as at present the battalion is
very short of officers. They were over the top about a week ago and
had about 17 officers killed and wounded, from which you will see
that it was some scrap. I was certainly lucky to be out of it. Capt.
Craig (my former company commander) was about the first to be
killed, while young MacArthur of B company got one through the
head. McDonald, also of B, got a leg off; another officer had the
whole of his jaw shot away. I think I would rather have the
other thing.[53]

By the way, my third pip is now through, so you may address me as 'Capting'. It is only 'acting' rank, while commanding a company, but I collect the nibs, which is important. The pay, I believe, is 13/6 per diem, and I now get groom allowance, and also an increase of 6p a day in my field allowance. As it is dated 24 June, I have a few quid of arrears to collect.

I don't know if I told you that our C.O. (Col. Jack) got a Brigade, and his successor, Major (now Lt.-Col.) Ritchie is wounded. I was very sorry that Col. Jack went away, as I was well on his right side. There is a rumour that another Cameronian, Col. Lee, D.S.O., is coming, and from all acounts he is a holy terror.[54] However, ça ne fait rien! News is absolutely top-hole these days. Last night I got an official message that Bulgaria had surrendered, and I'm keeping it as a souvenir. I hope to get a few more like it shortly, and there certainly seems some chance of that . . . . Today there are several excellent rumours: (1) 31,000 prisoners in the Ypres area and all our old hunting-ground of last winter re-taken (2) Cambrai and St. Quentin taken (3) Austria wanting peace. The last is a periodical one but may well be true now . . . .

[Crossing the Escaut Canal between Ossus and Honnecourt early on 5 October, the 1st Battalion advanced that day to La Terrière and the Hindenburg Support Line, where on 8 October Major Ritchie briefly reassumed command; he was again wounded the next day. The 19th Brigade steadily advanced throughout October in the face of determined opposition, through Dehéries, Bertry, Malincourt, Troisvilles, and Vendegies Wood, reaching Englefontaine on 24 October. The minimum reserve had rejoined the 1st Battalion on 12 October. Lt.-Col. Lee, Major Ritchie, and Major John Kirkwood successively commanded the battalion for brief periods; Lt.-Col. Hyde-Smith took command on 4 November.]

[Beaulencourt]
7 October, 1918

I am still at rear echelon, and as we have been in the same place now for nearly a week (although the line has been advanced several miles), we have settled down and made ourselves comfortable. I have a much improved dugout with bed, chair and table, and shall probably get it up to a high degree of comfort just before we move, or I get my orders to go up.

Since last writing, a new C.O. has arrived and departed, viz. Lt.-Col. Lee, D.S.O. – a Cameronian. If you wish to imagine him, he is exactly like Col. Fitzshrapnel in the well-known jam-tin picture by Bairnsfather. He was two days with us, and then was given one of the other battalions, which lost its C.O. in the last show. Major Ritchie is getting our battalion, and I am very glad of it. He is a fine chap and I get along well with him. He is here just now (also back from hospital); the only other officer is the R.C. chaplain. I had a talk with Major Ritchie the other night, and found that he is a director of the London Life (Trouncer's company), and quite an authority on life insurance.[55] By the way, the Brigadier gave me a special allotment of leave on account of my illness, but I refused it, as I want to arrange for Marjorie to come to France again. It rather looks as though I were one of the lucky ones these days.

Weather here is cold and blowy for the most part; at the moment it is raining, but in such comfortable quarters we have nothing to complain of. Our Division has been advancing all week, and the Bosche has been fleeing hurriedly, leaving all sorts of things behind him – including, incidentally, 24 men of one of our battalions whom he had taken prisoner: they had all been done in before being left. The Bosche certainly is a swine. I wouldn't like to be among the first lot of them we take, as the men were considerably annoyed. Meanwhile it's interesting to note how this is gradually becoming a back area. Only ten days ago the battalion was in the line just about here; now the broad-gauge railway is running several miles forward of it, and we have a casualty clearing station in the village (sic) with real nurses. I picked up a copy of the 'Kolnische Zeitung' lying in one house today; all the streets have been re-named by the Germans, but they've seen the last of it, except as prisoners.

[? Troisvilles]
11 October, 1918

Since last writing you I have been having some new experiences of war, i.e., following up a retreating enemy. The word 'retreating' is mild, though, as in the past 48 hours we have advanced 25 miles and the only resistance has been an occasional machine gun post covering the withdrawal. We've completely passed the old battle zone and crossed the Hindenburg Line, now miles behind us.

The villages we passed through today have civilians in them and are hardly damaged at all, having been right away back of the Bosche lines and well out of the war. Last night we stopped at a village which had been evacuated at eleven the previous morning. The streets had all been sown with mines; but fortunately some of the German engineers who fixed them up were captured, and when we left this morning they were going round under escort picking them out again – that's the stuff to give them. Today we have landed up at a good-sized village which the Bosche held yesterday evening at five, which gives you an idea of how closely we are on their heels. In fact, some cavalry and another Brigade have passed us, and are now 15 kilometres ahead. I have an A1 billet in 'Kaiser Wilhelm Strasse' (according to the Bosche) which was occupied by artillery officers, and I've picked up for a souvenir an artillery map that shows all the dispositions of our Division, with the names of every battalion marked in, dated only a few days ago. If we could carry all the stuff there are tons of souvenirs, as there is a Bosche Q.M. store in this street with all kinds of things in it. But we are travelling light, and the officers as well as the men have nothing but what can be carried by each man.

The roads all the way up are a perfect sight – streams of traffic of every description, troops, guns, ambulances, prisoners (we passed a convoy of 1500 to 2000 prisoners yesterday, all looking pretty miserable; and no wonder, they must be having the very deuce of a time). A whole Brigade of the Guards passed us today, going up on buses, and that presumably means business. In fact, altogether it is 'the goods'. The French civilians all have their flags out, the first time in four years. Our interpreter kisses them all as we go along. I tell you, old man, you're missing some show over here! I am still with the transport and, in fact, am the only officer with the reserve; otherwise I should be sure to go up to the company, and I probably will anyway very soon. But they must have some officers here. However, it's only a mile or two behind, so that I can easily catch up when I have to.

It was interesting to see the machine gun posts of the Bosche rear guards – just a little emplacement on each side of the road with a gun and a few boxes of 'ammo', and usually one or two dead Bosches besides them. The cleaning-up process hasn't reached here yet. Some of the guns were chalked, 'captured by 19 Brigade'.

[Malincourt]
17 October, 1918

Just now we are having a short rest in one of the recaptured villages. It is in quite decent condition, although there are still a few dead Bosches in the vicinity, awaiting burial; and we have a good house for a mess. No glass in the windows, but there is a piano. Capt. Forsyth (my second-in-command)[56] is an A1 player, and gives us some great recitals. I expect we'll be going on up again in a few days; if the troops keep going the way our Division did, we'll have some distance to go. Just now infantry has to keep off the roads as there is a terrific amount of traffic, getting everything shifted up. It is a hard job taking a company across country. Of course it's simplified by the fact that we can go straight across everything, crops and so on, and then there's always the pleasurable excitement of finding out if the village you've arrived at is the one you started out for.

I have applied for leave from November 3. If all goes well I'm going to meet Marjorie at Hendaye, near the Spanish frontier. We'll probably spend the whole time there, as I believe it's quite a nice little place. Of course at this time of year the climate down there should be just right for a holiday. In fact Biarritz is within an hour or two of the town, so we might take a day or two there as well. But much may happen before then, although I don't worry about that. Out here one gets into the habit of being quite happy if the next few meals and a night's rest are fairly sure . . . .

[Troisvilles]
20 October, 1918

I'm just writing now as I may not be able to write for a bit. We have moved up closer behind the line, and I expect will be going into the battle tonight or tomorrow morning. There was an attack [by the 17th and 38th Divisions] early this morning which I believe was very successful; prisoners have been coming through all morning. It is a drizzling wet day, and they are a very woebegone crowd, some of them wounded, all very miserable – and no wonder. I believe our Division is now carrying on the attack, and we are all ready, just awaiting orders. It depends a good deal on what happened this morning as to what sort of a show we'll have. If the Bosche was badly beaten we may have a running fight, chasing him back to his next holding place. He has been making a bit of a stand round here; but I don't think it will last now.

It is rather curious here, with our guns all round the village and troops all over the place, and an occasional shell coming in, to see the civilians going to church. They certainly are a courageous lot.

One old man told me he had heard nothing of his four sons since 1916, and the Bosche wouldn't allow him to write to them.

I was awakened at 2 a.m. by the barrage, and judging by the sound Fritz was getting 'particular hell'. Our guns get up marvellously quickly now, and I certainly think we have the right idea of keeping going. News is fine from other fronts, especially the north, which I know very well.

> *[The 1st Battalion crossed the river Selle on the evening of 22 October, and for the next four days steadily advanced, confronted chiefly by German machine-gunners, through Vendegies Wood to the outskirts of Englefontaine, which was finally taken in the early hours of 26 October. The battalion was withdrawn to Troisvilles that night, having sustained some 200 casualties in five days.]*

[Troisvilles]
27 October, 1918

Since last writing you I have been in some heavy fighting, during which our Division distinguished itself by advancing some 8 or 9 miles across open country against pretty severe opposition. We were relieved last night, and came back to billets, where we expect to have the best part of a week to rest. Perhaps some details of the fighting will be of interest to you.

We kicked off from the existing 'outpost line' at 2 a.m. on Wednesday morning, after a heavy barrage. During the barrage we had lively retaliation from the Bosche, and my friend Nicol was badly wounded right at the start. When we did move, we got right through the enemy's front defences, and in the first few minutes our Brigade had taken a few hundred prisoners, and polished off a good many others. We carried right on after Fritz, picking up stragglers and all sorts of stuff en route; but ultimately came up against him in force, in a defended position on a high bank at the other side of a thick wood. I was among the front line companies at that point, but in broad daylight; before the artillery came up it was impossible to oust him, as whenever we showed up in the open he started a terrific machine gun fire, and we had a lot of casualties. We remained under cover of the wood all night – and I can tell you it wasn't half cold as I hadn't even my coat with me and of course

161

we had no hot food – then at four next morning our field guns were up, as well as the heavy M.G.'s, and with these they gave the Bosche position a fright, so that our Brigade got right over it and away again. We did another few kilos cleaning out villages, and having a pretty lively time.

When retreating, he leaves a couple of men and an M.G. at some commanding position, and they can do some damage too. We surprised one of these, coming right on it, round a corner of the road, and I had the satisfaction of chalking it up to our credit. I also personally took 15 prisoners; they were all together in a post and evidently didn't know what was happening; if they had, they would have hopped it before then. However, they all put up their hands without the least unpleasantness, so it was too easy.[57] We were pulled up the second day, much the same as the first, by a strong position, but I had to have a shot at it, and I honestly thought my number was up as his machine gun bullets were hissing all round us, and ripping up the ground at my feet. I lost about half of the company, mostly wounded, and was lucky to get out of it myself. The position was taken next morning, after a barrage, by another Brigade of our own Division. We had a couple of tanks the second day, but I didn't see them do very much. Our C.O. (Col. Lee) was wounded the second day, as were about five other officers. So at the moment we are a bit reduced.

This village we have come back to was taken by the battalion some weeks ago, but it is now a peaceful spot, miles behind the line. I have quite a good billet and company mess, and while we are here will be quite comfortble. We got in about 2 a.m., and I slept until ten this morning. It was like 'a little bit of heaven', as for the last three days I never had an hour's consecutive sleep, and I was absolutely all in. Today I've been busy re-organizing, and checking deficiencies in equipment – some job for a Sunday, but of course we have to do that right away. This place is chock-a-block with troops, and there are about three different bands, so the natives are having a treat. There was some mail waiting for me, including a large packet of magazines, and both parts of *Bleak House* – for which thanks very much. The magazines are a godsend, as even though this is a civilised area, we can get nothing here; it's the other side of the old 'war belt', and communications are only being organized from our side. Of course, we have the Divisional canteen, but they don't have books and magazines, so yours are very much appreciated.

JOSEPH BROTHERTON MACLEAN

*[Crossing the Sambre on 6 November, the 1st
Battalion advanced eastward through Petit Mau-
beuge and Dourleurs, reaching the Dourleurs-
Eclaibes road in the late afternoon of 7 November;
heavy shelling and persistent machine-gun fire
hampered this advance. Next day the battalion
was withdrawn to Sabaras, on the eastern edge of
the Forest of Mormal.]*

[Sabaras]
9 November, 1918

We just came out of the line yesterday for a couple of days after
the most strenuous time I've had since I've been in this d_____
war. We have been in the big push, and our Brigade has done some
great work, its own share of the advance in the past three days
being something like 7 or 8 miles through forests and across rivers
and open country. What was not successful was the weather,
which has been wicked. You have no idea of what the men have
had to endure in discomfort, cold and wet, and general misery.

We kicked off on Monday morning – so did the rain, which started as a steady drizzle, then increased to a downpour that lasted
intermittently for three days and nights. As our fighting equipment
includes a sleeveless leather jerkin, but no greatcoat, we were all
soaked through right at the start. The approaches to the river
which we had to cross became a marsh that took us up to the knees
in water, so we were distinctly *wet*. So were the rations, and
altogether I thought half of us might die from exposure, but it's
wonderful what one can stand. My company was in front at the
beginning, and succeeded in taking its objective after fair resistance from M.G. fire and field guns, at close range. It was sufficiently exciting. During the advance I got a bullet right into my
respirator (which hangs in front of the chest). How it didn't go
through I don't know, but I suppose it was turned by some of the
metal parts of the respirator. Anyway, it's the nearest thing I've
had. Next day, we were in support to another company and had
only indirect trouble. The total extent of the advance and the
rapidity of it may be guessed from the fact that this village was in
the German lines on Monday, and is now a back area in ours. I
hear that the Bosche is still running, and I suppose we'll be on the
move again immediately.

On our way back we crossed the river on a pontoon bridge
which was being used for heavy transport and guns; but going out

we crossed it on planks and duck boards. It really is marvellous how all the branches of the army follow up behind the infantry so quickly. Already some of these small towns and villages look as if we had been in them for the duration. During the three days' fighting I had no shelter from weather, day or night, except a waterproof sheet, and slept (or tried to) on the ground – on the first and third nights at the edge of a wood, and on the second in a muddy hole where we had 'dug in' in the middle of a ploughed field. However, we survived it, and came through all right. My food was of the most ragtime description – wet bread and intensely filthy cheese, and once or twice a mess tin of tea made over a candle. But they all tasted good.

Since we came down yesterday at 2 a.m. we've had a regular beanfeast of comfort – hot meals, a warm bed, and a complete change into dry clothes. I can assure you the way to appreciate the minimum of comfort is to go without it for a few days. I have only one other officer with me in the company just now; last night we got a bottle of champagne and one of port from the Divisional canteen, so we had a considerable dinner. Then a great sleep, until about 8:30 this morning. Now I feel top-hole. Our interpreter says Germany's reply to our armistice terms will be in by Monday, so we have some hopes – perhaps – but certainly things are moving these days. Great events are happening. So although peace has seemed so far away, it may be coming at last.

[Sabaras]
10 November, 1918

I was very sorry indeed to hear of Craig's death, which is a great shock to me.[58] He was such a fine, vigorous fellow that one would never have thought he would go down. Please convey my sincere sympathy to Mrs. Craig. It certainly was fortunate about that insurance, and they should be fairly comfortably off. I was interested to hear details of the Actuarial Society meeting, and should like to read your paper. I'm very glad to hear that it was so well received.

Well, since I wrote last great things have been happening, and long before you get this you will know what the outcome is to be. Last night I got a message stating that we were awaiting Germany's response to our armistice terms, and that if these were accepted, we would remain in our present position (on the east side of Mormal Forest) for 28 days, then proceed to occupy a town on the Rhine. That's the stuff to give them. Today we heard of the Kaiser's abdication, so that generally everything in the garden is lovely. Even the weather has cleared up. Everyone is feeling in great form.

If this comes off all right, as we hope and expect, we shall probably have a picnic here for the 28 days, and we're lucky to be in billets. We fully expected to go back up the line today. But there is no word of such a move (except rapid moves to the rear by the enemy), and we are making up all our arrears of food and sleep, and general luxury and comfort. I have an application in for leave to Spain on December 15th – by which time it seems I have a good chance of being in Germany. But I hope I'll get it all right, and spend Christmas in Aguilas.

Another message we had today is one of congratulations from our Divisional Commander for our share in the recent operations, including the crossing of the Sambre. We certainly had a helluva time, and the Brigade did fine work.

Today we are having an easy day, and have nothing but church parade. I am going round to one of the other companies for tea; we are hoping that before the day is out we may hear Gemany's reply, and that it will be what we expect. Exciting times these are; but we do live . . . .

[Berlaimont]
13 November, 1918

Since I last wrote a few days ago, the armistice has been declared, and of course the effect on us is considerable. Instead of continuing the push, as we expected to do, we moved a short distance to this small town, where we are in billets. My company has 'clicked' for very good quarters, and personally I am very well off, having a room which was the permanent billet of a Bosche officer – an inspector of factories. It has a stove and a bed, mit sheets – très chic, and I can tell you it isn't half A1 to strike something good at last. There are lots of civilians here, and they are very pleased to see us, as they have been having a rotten time; if all they say is true, which I don't really doubt, the Bosche has been a proper swine.

I expect you will be pleased to hear that I have been recommended for the Military Cross. As a matter of fact, I'll probably not get it, as our Corps Commander is very sparing in the giving of medals. But in the meantime, I have had the customary card of congratulation from the Divisional General, which alleges that I 'distinguished myself in the field on 23-24 October'. That was when we took Vendegies Wood, and B company raked in some prisoners; but I didn't do anything special. However, it's always some satisfaction to be recommended, whether I get the M.C. or not – especially in one of the last battles of the war.

I don't know what our programme will be after the armistice, but I suppose it will be umpteen months before I can clear off.[59] However, I can stick that all right. We're getting the troops polished up and looking like peacetime soldiers again. I have some chance to get a decent company now that we'll have the same men for more than a few weeks at a time.

'But we do live'. Joseph B. Maclean in retirement at Yarmouthport, Massachusetts, c. 1960.

Notes to Letters

1. Of the officers so named who served with the 1st Battalion in 1917-1918, Lieut. R.G. Nicol is most probably the figure to whom these letters often refer. He was Maclean's best friend in the battalion: 'a congenial soul and we get along fine' (20 December, 1917). They had trained in Scotland with Territorial battalions; both were promoted to Lieutenant's rank as of 1 June, 1916. The two men were regularly in different companies but shared many experiences in and out of the line. The last allusion to Nicol (27 October, 1918) underscores a continuing regard: 'my friend Nicol was badly wounded right at the start' [of the advance through Vendegies Wood to Englefontaine].

2. Roderick Maclean (d. 1926) and his wife Margaret Chisholm Maclean (d. 1928), took a particular interest in their nephew's welfare during the war years. Their son, Captain Hector Maclean, M.C. (1896-1929), served with the 7th Battalion (and later the 5th Battalion) of The Cameronians.

   Salutation and conclusion of later letters are identical with those of the first and are therefore omitted, together with the regular notation, 'B.E.F.'.

3. An evocative account of the rigours of the Étaples 'Bull-Ring' makes part of the retrospective war-time narrative by Pte. W.A. Taylor, 1st Battalion, who observes, 'It was very strenuous, with dust, sweat, and fatigue making one feel like a wilted flower' (Liddle Collection, Leeds University Library).

   On the early development of gas helmet and box respirator see the memoir by Lieut. Leslie Barley, 1st Battalion (Liddle Collection); also Simon Jones, 'Gas Warfare: The British Defensive Measures, Part I: The Second Battle of Ypres', *Stand To!* 14, (Summer, 1985), 15-23.

4. I.e., Mills hand grenades. But the earlier 'jam-tins' were still in use at training camps in 1917. These were 'old jam-tins filled with explosives and a mixed assortment of scrap-iron, fitted with a short length of fuse which had to be lighted before thrown' (Captain I.D. Kennedy, 2nd Battalion, The Cameronians: 'Personal Narrative', Liddle Collection).

5. Captain Thomas R. McLellan (1883-1941). The Territorial's suspicion of regular officers as a class speaks through comments in this and the following letter. But later references acknowledge McLellan's professionalism (30 August, 1917).
6. The 2nd Royal Welch Fusiliers. Both Robert Graves and Siegfried Sassoon served with this regiment; see Sassoon's account of Cameronians in action at Croisilles in April of 1917, in *Siegfried Sassoon: Diaries 1915-1918*, ed. Rupert Hart-Davis (London, 1983), 154-155, and especially 'Memories of an Infantry Officer', in *The Memoirs of George Sherston* (Harrisburg, Pa., 1967), 435-445.
7. Major (later Lt.-Col.) Herbert Charles Hyde-Smith, D.S.O. and bar.
8. Bruce Bairnsfather (1885-1956), English illustrator and author who served with the British forces in the war, created the character of 'Old Bill' to typify the spirit of the British infantryman.
9. Probably Captain J.C.E. Hay, who had come to the 1st Battalion from the 6th (Territorial) Battalion.
10. Lt.-Col. J.C. Chaplin, D.S.O., had come to France with the 1st Battalion in August, 1914. He assumed command of the battalion in May, 1915. In November, 1917 he took command of the 103rd Brigade in the 34th Division.
11. The 'Kerensky Offensive' of 1-16 July, directed at Lemberg (Galicia), was checked well short of that city. On 19 July a massive German counter-attack crushed Russian forces on this front, driving them back in disorder to the Zbrucz river, some 40 miles east of their position on 1 July.
12. The persons named in this paragraph were, with one exception, actuarial associates and friends during the brothers' pre-war years in Glasgow. William Bannatyne (1876-1968) had a long and distinguished career, culminating in his appointment as Manager of the Scottish Temperance and General Assurance Company of Glasgow; he was President of the Faculty of Actuaries from 1940 to 1942, and Vice President of the Faculty thereafter, until 1948. Walter Denham (1876-1969), John Bowie (1880-1940), and William Ross, Jr. (1889-1967), all Fellows of the Faculty, became highly regarded members of their profession. James P. McNaught was 'senior clerk' at the Scottish Temperance for fifty years, until 1951.
13. This officer, often mentioned in these letters, duly became Signals Officer of the 1st Battalion.
14. Lieut. M.M.K. White, of the 5th Cameronians, had for some time been experimenting with the manufacture and use of

hand grenades.
15. It was Lt.-Col. Chaplin who took a second prize, on 'Ginger', in a competition for 'Officers' Chargers, 15 hands and under'. An amusing illustrated account of the occasion, held at Cavillon, and also of the Divisional race meeting in May at Ayette, near Arras, appear in Graham Seton Hutchison, *The Thirty-Third Division in France and Flanders 1915-1919* (London, 1921), 50-59.
16. Lieut. (A/Capt.) David Cameron Chisholm, M.C. (perhaps a cousin or nephew of Margaret Chisholm Maclean ['Aunt Maggie']) was commissioned on 30 January, 1915, and joined The Northamptonshire Regiment on 4 October of that year, serving as A/Captain from 14 October. He was awarded the M.C. for bravery in the Somme battle, on 16 August, 1916, and wounded on 26 September. He rejoined his regiment in mid-July, 1917, and was taken prisoner shortly thereafter. He survived the war; but details of his connection with Joseph and Alex Maclean are not known.
17. Lenox and Stockbridge, in the Berkshire Hills of Western Massachusetts, are some fifty miles west of Springfield, the home of Alex and Amy Maclean.
18. These battalions of The Highland Light Infantry (City of Glasgow Regiment), which made part of the 97th Brigade in the 32nd Division, had sustained heavy casualties in the German attack of 10 July.
19. Probably Lieut. H.G. Caldwell, who served with both regular battalions of The Cameronians.
20. Evander ('Bobbie') Mackenzie, one of the five sons of Mrs. Mackenzie (née MacLeod), a maternal great-aunt with whom the brothers spent summers in Stornoway before the war, enlisted in The Seaforth Highlanders shortly after July, 1916, and was posted to the 2nd Battalion. He was killed in action on 10 May, 1917, at the age of 38, near Fampoux (subsequently the site of the Seaforth Regimental Memorial). He is buried in the Étaples Military Cemetery. *The Stornoway Gazette* for 18 May, 1917, has a moving obituary, which observes that Mackenzie had served in Egypt at the time of the South African War, and that 'he was held in great esteem, both for his uprightness of character and his sterling qualities as a workman' [he was a stonemason].
21. On 24 August B company, led by Captain Edgar W. Sussex, M.C., had taken a German position ('Gelaide Post'). The next evening a German attack on B and D companies, and on units of the 20th Royal Fusiliers, re-took the post. Captain Sussex

was killed in the action of 25 August.

22. Robert Jeffrey (1884-1956), a Fellow of the Faculty of Actuaries, was employed by the Scottish Amicable Life Assurance Society in Edinburgh, London, and Glasgow. He eventually became the Secretary (i.e., deputy to the Manager) of that company.

23. A professional journal published monthly by the Massachusetts Mutual Life Insurance Company.

24. *The American Magazine*, published monthly in Springfield, Ohio, occasionally included articles on various aspects of insurance.

25. 2/Lieut. J. Preston. The D.S.O. was ordinarily awarded only to officers of 'field rank' and above.

26. Henry Moir (1871-1937), born in Scotland, was a Fellow of the Faculty of Actuaries. He came to the U.S.A. in 1901, joining the Home Life Insurance Company in New York City (where Alex Maclean was employed from 1909 to 1916), eventually becoming Vice President and Actuary of the company. Later he was President of the United States Life Insurance Company; in 1918 he was elected President of the Actuarial Society of America.

27. It has not been possible to identify this officer. The term 'knut' as a rule carries a slightly disparaging sense (echoing the English music-hall ballad of the period: 'I'm Gilbert the filbert, the king of the 'knuts'), but here signifies primarily 'a fashionable and socially well-connected young man'. Lady Diana Manners (1892-1987), central figure in a group of young aristocrats, many of whom were killed in France, was widely considered to be the most beautiful woman of her day. She worked as a nurse at Guy's Hospital in London throughout the war. In 1919 she married Duff Cooper, subsequently assuming the title of Viscountess Norwich.

28. Captain W.A. Parker, D.S.O., joined the 5th Battalion in France in early November, taking command of D company at that time, Educated in Glasgow, he became after the war a successful civil engineer, in South America and (from 1932) in Edinburgh. Major C.C. Scott, M.C., had commanded the 1st Battalion since 18 November, when Lt.-Col. Chaplin left to take command of the 103rd Brigade.

29. C and D companies occupied front line trenches at Passchendaele from 23-25 January.

30. 2/Lieut. Herbert W. Cole, 'one of the finest fellows I ever knew' (25 April, 1918), was a graduate of Glasgow High School. An accomplished musician who had studied with the Belgian

violinist Henri Verbrugghen (1873-1934), Cole was first violinist in the Scottish Orchestra, and conductor of the Glasgow Amateur Orchestral Society. He was killed in action on 14 April, 1918. About this time letters, omitted here, begin to reflect Maclean's friendly association also with Captain William T. Craig, who commanded D company. Born in Turnberry, Craig became mathematical master at Hutcheson's Grammar School in Glasgow before enlisting as a private in 1914. He was killed in action on 21 September, 1918.

31. John S. Thompson (1884-1979), a Canadian, was Maclean's immediate superior in the Actuarial Department of the Mutual Life Insurance Company, in New York City, from 1911 to 1925, when Thompson joined the Mutual Benefit Life Insurance Company. He was President of the Mutual Benefit from 1946 until his retirement in 1953. The 'extracts from my letters' refer to the letter of 30 August, 1917, which was presumably forwarded by Alex Maclean to Thompson for reproduction in *The Mutual Life Quarterly.*

32. Cascara sagrada, derived from buckthorn tree bark, is a powerful laxative.

33. At the Divisional level of this competition, Maclean's platoon defeated platoons from the 2nd Worcestershires (100th Brigade) and the 2nd Argyll and Sutherland Highlanders (98th Brigade). Major-General R.J. Pinney, C.B., commanded the 33rd Division at this time; Brigadier C.R.G. Mayne, D.S.O., commanded the 19th Brigade. The photograph has been lost.

34. Lt.-Col. Frederick S. Draffen, D.S.O. (1880-1955), a veteran of Spion Kop, came to France as Adjutant of the 6th Scottish Rifles. Wounded on 15 June, 1915, he subsequently commanded the 13th Royal Sussex in England for a time. He then served in France as Chief Instructor at the Fifth Army Infantry School before his posting to the 2nd Battalion. He assumed command of the 1st Battalion on 25 March, 1918.

35. Lieut. William E. Brodie was killed in action on 29 March, 1918.

36. A variety of sultana raisin cake, Welsh in origin, baked in the form of a loaf. Welsh troops sent to the Kashmir and Khyber station in India added cold tea to the basic recipe, giving the final product a distinctive flavour.

37. During this 'special leave', it appears that Maclean and his cousin Marjorie had planned to be married in Paris. They had known each other since childhood, although Marjorie was born (in 1895) and brought up in Aguilas, Spain (with

occasional early visits to Scotland), where her father, Norman Maclean, owned a business that processed esparto grass for export. In 1908 his wife, Jessica Stephens Maclean, brought her two eldest children to Scotland, to be educated in Glasgow. Allan, who was to be killed at Gallipoli in 1915, was enrolled at Glasgow High School; Marjorie at Miss Bunting's School in Hyndland. In the course of time, certainly by 1911, when Maclean emigrated to the U.S.A., it was understood that the cousins would marry when he was established in New York. The war delayed but did not alter that arrangement. Marjorie remained in Aguilas for the greater part of the war, then in June, 1918, the marriage took place in Paris. See 30 May, 1918 *et seq.*

38. A useful overview of the confused events described in this letter may be found in H.H. Story, M.C., *History of The Cameronians (Scottish Rifles) 1910-1933* (Aylesbury, 1961), 283-289.

39. 'Lt.-Col. Draffen sent 'D' Company to stiffen [the] front' (Story, 285) between Merris and the western outskirts of Meteren, then manned chiefly by exhausted and shaken troops from the 31st, 34th, and 50th Divisions. As this letter states, Cole was killed on 14 April; Lieut. W.M. Anderson was wounded the next day. The other officer was probably Lieut. W.D. Roger.

40. 'Early on the morning of the 19th the [19th] Brigade was placed at the disposal of the 34th Division and moved to the vicinity of St. Jans Cappel in reserve to meet an expected attack' (Story, 289).

41. Lieut. F.T. Goble, M.C.

42, Lieut. T.O. Thorburn and Lieut. J.B. Loudon were killed in action on 13 April. These two officers 'were baptized [in St. John's United Presbyterian Church, Hamilton] on the same day, received commissions in the same battalion of the Scottish Rifles, went to the front about the same time, and fell in battle on the same day' (*Glasgow Evening Citizen*, 23 April, 1918).

43. Lt.-General Sir Herbert Plumer, later Field Marshal, 1st Baron Plumer of Messines and of Bilton, commanded 2nd Army at this time.

44. Maclean had enlisted as a private when he arrived from America in 1914. The 'old ranker' is unidentified. The other officer was probably 2/Lieut. W. Chambers, gazetted to that rank as of 2 April, 1917.

45. See Genesis xix: 26.

46. The bride-to-be and her mother, Jessica Stephens Maclean travelled together from the family residence in Aguilas, Spain, to Bordeaux, where they met Maclean, who escorted them to Paris. The marriage took place on 19 June.
47. Major Richard D. Hunter, D.S.O. and bar; Lieut. Cecil Wigan, who later became Adjutant of the 1st Battalion.
48. The Rev. Augustus J. Kesting performed the marriage in the Scottish Church at 17, rue Bayard (precursor of the 'Scots Kirk', erected in 1959 at the same address). 'Dickson' is probably Hugh S. Dickson, eldest son of Mr. Jno. R.D. Dickson, whose three sons attended Glasgow High School when Maclean and his brother were there. 'Douglas' is unidentified. A characteristically terse cablegram to Alex duly confirmed the marriage: 'Married today. Lieut. Maclean'.
49. Hargrove Bellamy (1896-   ), born in Wilmington, North Carolina, attended the University of North Carolina; in 1917 he was the first student at that institution to enlist in the American Army. As one of the Advanced School Detachment sent to France to prepare for the arrival of his American unit, he was attached to B company of the 1st Battalion. Later he commanded a company in the 199th Infantry, 30th American Division. He was wounded and taken prisoner on 29 September, 1918, during the American drive against the Hindenburg Line. For 'extraordinary heroism' in action he was awarded the Distinguished Service Cross. After the war he became the mayor of Wilmington. He also served with the American forces in the war of 1939-1945.
50. Major the Hon. Harold Ritchie, D.S.O. and bar, after service in Salonika, volunteered for service in France, joining the 1st Battalion in September, 1917. His father, Charles Thomson Ritchie, 1st Baron Ritchie of Dundee (1838-1906), was Balfour's Secretary of the Exchequer in 1902-1903.
51. On 8 August ('the black day of the German Army', in Ludendorff's phrase) the British Fourth and French Fifth Armies mounted a large-scale and brilliantly successful offensive between Amiens and Rheims.
52. Lt.-Col. Jack took a poor view of this affair, but seems not to have held Lieut. Maclean accountable: 'a patrol of six men under 2/Lieut. F. has been ambushed by a party of Germans. Two of my men are killed, one is missing, and two are wounded. F's patrol seems to have regarded its mission too lightly, and to have taken insufficient precautions' (*General Jack's Diary 1914-1918*, ed. John Terraine [London, 1964], 253).

53. Captain Craig, 2/Lieut. D.R. MacArthur and Lieut. H.S. McDonald were all killed on 21 September.
54. Lt.-Col. H.H. Lee, D.S.O., was thrice wounded in the course of his service with both regular battalions of The Cameronians (Scottish Rifles).
55. In civilian life a partner with the banking firm of Brightwen and Company, London, Harold Ritchie had been a Director of the London Life Association, Ltd., since 1913. Harold M. Trouncer (1871-1948), Actuary of the London Life, was elected President of the Institute of Actuaries in 1930.

    Shortly after 7 October, Harold Ritchie was again wounded; 'but he refused, owing to the lack of officers, to take advantage of the opportunity [to take leave]. He was therefore immediately attached to the 1st Queen's as C.O. He was gravely wounded again, and died at the clearing station on his way from the firing line ... he was familiarly known [by his men] as "the fighting colonel", (*London Times,* 19 November, 1918).
56. Captain J.W. Forsyth, originally with the 6th Battalion.
57. Maclean was awarded the Military Cross for his role in this affair.
58. 'Craig' is unidentified. He was probably one of the group of young Scottish professional men with whom Maclean associated in New York City before the war.
59. Joseph B. Maclean was officially struck off the strength of the 1st Battalion in July, 1919, and of the 7th Battalion (his original gazetting in January, 1915) on 20 January, 1921. He returned to his position with the Mutual Life, in New York City, in the spring of 1919.

Acknowledgements

Many people have helped me with this part of the book. I am particularly grateful to Lieutenant-Colonel Sir John Baynes, whose wise and friendly presence has been a steadying influence on every aspect of the undertaking. To work with him has been an honour and a distinct pleasure.

The late Brigadier D.B. Riddell-Webster gave me much useful assistance during the few months of our acquaintance. I count myself fortunate to have met with him in Hamilton during the summer of 1986, and to have profited in many ways from his sensible counsel. A generosity akin to his informed the help provided after his death by Major Peter J. Eydes, King's Own Scottish Borderers (formerly of The Cameronians); Mr. John McGourty, Custodian of the Regimental Museum in Hamilton; and in particular Mr. William G.F. Boag, sometime Assistant to the Keeper, Scottish United Services Museum in Edinburgh, now Curatorial Consultant to the Regimental Museum Committee.

Mr. Peter T. Scott, Honorary Editor, *Stand To!* and Colonel Peter Stromberg, United States Military Academy, West Point, New York, were very helpful when the project was first getting under way. Subsequently Professor Brian Bond, Department of War Studies, King's College, University of London, kindly read and evaluated the unrevised manuscript. At a later stage Professor Dewitt Ellinwood, State University of New York at Albany, read a revised version of the letters; as did Professor Andrew Rutherford, Warden of Goldsmiths' College in the University of London, who gave me valuable editorial advice. To all these scholars and soldiers I am very much indebted.

I am grateful for the opportunity to consult manuscript and other material made available by Dr. Elizabeth M.H. Smith and the staff of the Public Record Office (Kew); by Mr. Peter Simkins and the staff of the Research and Information Office (and the Department of Photography) at the Imperial War Museum; by Mr. D.L. McCallum, Librarian of the Social Science Department in the Mitchell Library, Glasgow; and by Mr. Peter Liddle, Curator of The Liddle Collection in the Leeds University Library (formerly located at Sunderland Polytechnic), together with his congenial staff. I must also acknowledge the assistance of the Army Records Centre, Hayes, Middlesex, and of the Commonwealth War Graves Commission, Maidenhead.

I owe a great debt to the Director of University Libraries at the State University of New York at Albany for providing me with office space to work on the book; and I wish to acknowledge in particular the tireless efficiency of Sally Stevenson and Gwen Deiber of the Inter-Library Loan Office in the Main Library at Albany.

Mr. Walter Klem, my father's closest associate and friend at the Mutual Life Insurance Company in New York over a period of many years, has kindly provided much information bearing on their years together, for which I am most grateful. My thanks are due also to Mr. William Morrison, President, The Faculty of Actuaries in Scotland; Mr. C.D.A. Mackie, Secretary-General, The Institute of Actuaries, London; Mr. J.M. Macharg, General Secretary, The Scottish Provident Institution, Edinburgh; Mr Douglas McKinnon, sometime General Manager, The Scottish Mutual Assurance Society, Glasgow; and Mr. W.B. McBride, Actuary, The London Life Association, Ltd., Bristol. To meet with Mr. Morrison and with Mr. McKinnon and to share their memories of my father has been a very special privilege. I am grateful also to Miss Donna Richardson, Research Librarian, The Society of Actuaries, Itasca, Illinois; Mr John Rich, Staff Historian, Mutual Life Archives, Washington, D.C.; Mr. Guy McLain, Jr., Archivist of The Massachusetts Mutual Life Insurance Company, Springfield, Massachusetts; and Mr. Robert Sparrow, Archives, The Sun Life Assurance Company, Toronto.

For information bearing on details in the letters, I am indebted to Mr. Alan Cunningham, Chief Librarian, Western Isles Libraries, and Mr. Ian Horne, Outer Hebrides Tourist Board, both of Stornoway, Isle of Lewis; Colonel R.C. Jeffrey, T.D., D.L., Curator, Museum of The Northamptonshire Regiment, Northampton; Mr. Philip Ziegler, London; Reverend Bruce Robertson, The Scots Kirk, Paris; Dr. Claude Bissell and Professor Desmond Morton, both of the University of Toronto; Mrs. T. Dobroslavic, Vancouver Public Library, Vancouver, British Columbia; Mr. Robert Quist, Utica Public Library, Utica, New York; Mr. Hargrove Bellamy, Wilmington, North Carolina, and Ms. Joan Spencer, Cameron Village Regional Library, Raleigh, North Carolina; Mrs. M. Sweeney, Culinary Institute of America, Hyde Park, New York;

and Mr. D. St. John-Grubb, Poughkeepsie, New York.

The Rector of The High School of Glasgow, Mr. Robin G. Easton, M.A., generously and hospitably provided me with invaluable copies of school records from my father's time. For information bearing on the years before and immediately after the war I am much indebted to Mr. Colin Maclean, Poole, Hants; Mr. Fitzroy D. Maclean, New York City; and Mr. Dermid Maclean, Sun City Center, Florida.

I am lastingly grateful to my late sister Elizabeth, from whom I received letters in the spring of 1986. Her knowledge and understanding of our father was discerning and subtle: deeply rooted in sympathetic regard, and love. A personal memoir from her hand was to have introduced the edited letters; but her untimely death in 1987 cancelled that prospect. Subsequently her husband, Dr. Henry Slayter, winnowed out from her papers and gave to me many irreplaceable documents and photographs bearing on Maclean family history. I thank him for his constant support, and for his generous contribution to the enterprise. He and I agree that this portion of the book should be dedicated to Elizabeth Cameron Maclean Slayter.

My thanks are due also to Michael Dubiac for his help with the map of France and Flanders 1914-1918 (based on a map in H.H. Story, *History of The Cameronians [Scottish Rifles] 1910-1933;* Aylesbury, 1961).

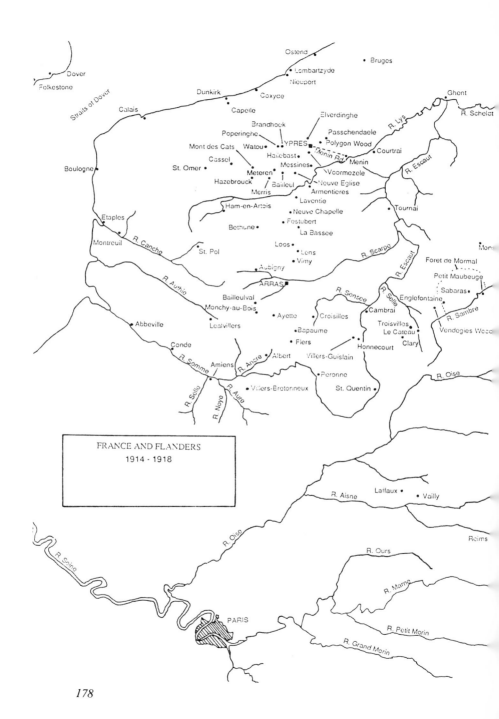

FRANCE AND FLANDERS
1914 - 1918

178